God

Three Who Are One

Joseph A. Bracken, SJ

Tatha Wiley, Series Editor

A Michael Glazier Book

LITURGICAL PRESS
Collegeville, Minnesota

www.litpress.org

A Michael Glazier Book published by Liturgical Press

Cover design by Ann Blattner

1   2   3   4   5   6   7   8   9

Library of Congress Cataloging-in-Publication Data

Bracken, Joseph A.
    God : three who are one / Joseph A. Bracken.
        p.   cm. — (Engaging theology : Catholic perspectives)
    Includes bibliographical references and index.
    ISBN: 978-0-8146-5990-8
        1. Trinity.   I. Title.

BT111.3.B73 2008
231'.044—dc22

2008004759

CONTENTS

Editor's Preface

In calling the Second Vatican Council, Pope John XXIII challenged those he gathered to take a bold leap forward. Their boldness would bring a church still reluctant to accept modernity into full dialogue with it. The challenge was not for modernity to account for itself, nor for the church to change its faith, but for the church to transform its conception of faith in order to speak to a new and different situation.

Today we stand in a postmodern world. The assumptions of modernity are steeply challenged, while the features of postmodernity are not yet fully understood. Now another world invites reflection and dialogue, and the challenge is to discover how the meanings and values of Christian faith speak effectively to this new situation.

This series takes up the challenge. Central concerns of the tradition—God, Jesus, Scripture, Anthropology, Church, and Discipleship—here are lifted up. In brief but comprehensive volumes, leading Catholic thinkers lay out these topics with a historically conscious eye and a desire to discern their meaning and value for today.

Designed as a complete set for an introductory course in theology, individual volumes are also appropriate for specialized courses. Engaging Theology responds to the need for teaching resources alive to contemporary scholarly developments, to the current issues in theology, and to the real questions about religious beliefs and values that people raise today.

Tatha Wiley
Series Editor

Introduction

Faith and Ultimate Reality

To a little child reading the Baltimore Catechism, the answer to the question, "Who made me?" is easy: "God made me." But if the child were further to ask, "Who made God?" there is apparently no answer. Nobody made God because God is by definition uncreated; God is the Creator of everything else that exists. Yet even God must have a reason to exist. On the contrary, you may say, God has no reason to exist; God simply is. God, in the eyes of Christians and other theists, is Ultimate Reality. Ultimate Reality simply is; one cannot logically ask why it is the way that it is. Otherwise it would not be Ultimate Reality, that which exists before everything else and upon which everything else depends.

Another way to think about Ultimate Reality is to ask how the world began. When the astrophysicist Edwin Hubble in 1929 noticed the so-called red shift in light coming from distant galaxies, he established empirically what had been theoretically predicted on the basis of Albert Einstein's theory of general relativity: the universe is expanding in all directions.[1]

But if the universe is continually expanding, then it must have begun long ago from equivalently a zero point in terms of space and time. One astrophysicist, Fred Hoyle, sarcastically referred to it as the "big bang" theory for the origin of the universe, but to Hoyle's exasperation (since he favored a different "steady state" understanding of the universe), the term caught on and is commonly used today to explain the origin of

---

[1] See Ian G. Barbour, *Religion and Science: Historical and Contemporary Issues* (San Francisco: HarperCollins, 1997), 195.

the universe.[2] But does it really explain how the world began or does the big bang itself need further explanation?

Nancey Murphy and George F. R. Ellis, in their book *On the Moral Nature of the Universe*, argue that there are five possibilities for the origin of the universe: random chance, high probability, necessity, universality, and design.[3] Random chance says in effect that there is no explanation; the universe just happened. High probability and necessity both suffer from the fact that we have no way of comparing our universe with other real or possible universes so as to judge the degree of probability or the necessity of our own universe. Universality presupposes that sooner or later everything that can happen will happen; so our universe is presumably just one of many universes that either have existed, exist right now, or will some day exist. Design insists that the universe in its "fine-tuning" is too complicated to be anything else but the work of a transcendent intelligence, in effect, a Creator God, who set up the physical laws and the initial boundary conditions for both the big bang and the subsequent development of the universe.

For our purposes, what is important here is to realize that whatever option one chooses regarding the origins of the universe, it is always made on the basis of an act of faith. That is, there is no way to prove that one option is right and that the others are mistaken. Yet the act of faith is different, depending upon the option that one chooses. If one, for example, chooses the first option, namely, that the universe originated by random chance, one's act of faith is relatively impersonal. I believe that this is the way things are; there is no higher purpose or direction in the way the world functions. Whatever purpose or direction that exists in my own life is of my own design. I simply choose to live one way rather than another and I hope that it will work out, at least for me personally. On the contrary, if I put my faith in a Creator God who designed the universe as a whole and has given me a place within it, then my act of faith is more personal. I am not simply trusting that something is the case; I am trusting in a higher power in my life, a Creator God who cares for me personally.

Where does one get the courage to make that second act of faith? I would argue that it is due in no small measure to the way that one is raised and educated. If my parents and teachers themselves believe in

---

[2] Ibid., 198–99.

[3] Nancey Murphy and George F. R. Ellis, *On the Moral Nature of the Universe: Theology, Cosmology, and Ethics* (Minneapolis: Fortress, 1996), 53–59.

God and communicate to me their own faith through word and action, I will almost certainly follow their lead until something happens to make me question the faith of my parents and teachers. At that point I will have to decide for myself whether or not to continue to believe in the existence of God. This is the transition from the faith of a child to the faith of a young adult. It happens sooner or later to every young person, even though the temptation remains strong in many cases to ignore the question out of fear of making a mistake or because of social pressure from others. In the end, however, one comes to a personal decision on this matter, either through thinking it out for oneself or in virtue of a religious experience, a deeply felt encounter with the Sacred (God?) at some point in one's life. Sometimes it is the result of a combination of the two.

Since the rest of this book will be presenting a rational argument for belief in God as triune, a community of divine persons, I will offer here some thoughts on the other possibility of coming to believe in God, namely, having a felt interpersonal experience of God. In his widely read book *I and Thou*, Martin Buber noted that we humans live for the most part in what he called a "I-It" world.[4] That is, we unconsciously treat not just things but even other people as objects to be dealt with according to our own interests and desires. We have no personal interest, for example, in the person at the checkout counter in the supermarket nor are they especially interested in us except as another customer in the middle of a long day. But we do have in varying degrees personal relations with some people (family members, good friends, etc.). These people by their interpersonal communication with us lift us into another world according to Buber, the world of "I-Thou," at least at intervals.[5] We sense that we are special to them, and that they are special to us. But Buber also claims that every time we genuinely say "Thou" to another human being we are also experiencing the divine "Thou" within the human "Thou."[6] So the experience of God as a personal Other is not that rare; we simply do not pay much attention to it when it happens because our attention is focused on another human being.

In addition, most people can testify that at still other moments of their life they felt the presence of God. As Rudolph Otto notes in his

---

[4] Martin Buber, *I and Thou*, 2nd ed., trans. Ronald Gregor Smith (New York: Scribner's, 1958), 3–4.

[5] Ibid.

[6] Ibid., 6.

classic work *The Idea of the Holy*, this is not always a pleasant experience; it can also be frightening.[7] We can feel a glow within as we witness a brilliant sunset and are brought to reflect on God's goodness to us in the gifts of creation. But we can also feel overwhelmed as we witness a violent storm at sea, a tornado, or other natural catastrophe and reflect on the power of nature and nature's God. But in either case God is no longer simply an idea in our minds but a dominant personal presence much greater than ourselves. Psychologists can tell us that we are suffering from an illusion, that what we are experiencing has a perfectly logical naturalistic explanation. But for many of us when it happens, it is a far more convincing argument for the existence of God than any possible line of rational argument.

Yet, in fairness to the secular psychologists, we should also recognize that not every "voice" that speaks to us out of the depths of our unconscious is the voice of God. Masters of the spiritual life like the founder of the Society of Jesus (the Jesuits), St. Ignatius of Loyola, have carefully analyzed the various "movements" within human minds and hearts and laid down rules for the "discernment of spirits."[8] Ignatius himself believed in the existence of the devil as a malicious personal being who works in our minds and hearts in a manner opposite to the Holy Spirit. So his rules may seem a bit quaint to modern readers. But the inner conflict and anxiety that people sometimes experience during the process of conversion is real enough, whether one believes in the devil as the source of one's temptation or simply feels that one is dealing with long-repressed personal feelings and desires.

Ignatius of Loyola proposes a convenient rule of thumb for people who find it hard to decide which "voice" they are hearing. If one's life is a mess because of bad habits or harmful relationships, then the "voice" of God in these circumstances is usually insistent that it is time to make some changes. Don't delay any longer; act now. The "voice" of the evil spirit or one's own subconscious, on the contrary, urges caution and delay. It will be too hard to change. Besides, everyone else is acting the same way, and so forth.[9] Yet, says Ignatius, once an individual has gone through a conversion experience and seen the error of his or her ways,

---

[7] Rudolf Otto, *The Idea of the Holy: An Inquiry into the Non-rational Factor in the Idea of the Divine and Its Relation to the Rational*, trans. John W. Harvey (New York: Oxford University Press, 1958), 12–40.

[8] *The Spiritual Exercises of Saint Ignatius*, trans. George E. Ganss, SJ (Chicago: Loyola University Press, 1992), 189–95.

[9] Ibid., 121–25.

then the tactics of the Holy Spirit and the evil spirit are reversed. Now God is urging the individual to stay the course, not to become discouraged because of unexpected difficulties encountered along the way. The evil spirit, on the contrary, plays on one's fears and anxieties about the future, suggesting that it is futile to behave this way. In the end, it will be too difficult and one will be forced to give up.[10]

Ignatius also proposes that one should not make potentially serious or long-range decisions quickly and while under stress.[11] The Holy Spirit frequently needs time to bring us to a deep sense of peace and a strong feeling of certitude about what to do next. The evil spirit, on the contrary, will in similar circumstances urge us to decide quickly on the basis of the feelings of the moment. Why wait? If it feels good, just do it! Don't worry about the future; the future will take care of itself. Ignatius would likewise suggest that, depending upon the seriousness of the decision to be made, one should talk the matter out with a trusted friend, counselor, priest, or minister before coming to a final decision. The other person can help us see ourselves and our situation in a more objective light even if they have nothing specific to recommend.

To sum up, then, the study of theology is seldom, if ever, purely academic. After all, one is probing into the ultimate meaning and value of one's life, realizing that Ultimate Reality, however one conceives it, will always be somewhat distant and mysterious, requiring an act of faith in some form or other. But at the same time, no decision that one makes in the course of a lifetime is more important for one's self-identity or sense of purpose in life. Hence, as we go through the various chapters of this book, studying the history of the doctrine of God within the Christian tradition and noting its relevance for our own lives here and now, it will be good to pray as well as to think, at least at intervals to reflect on the personal significance of what we study for the conduct of our lives. In this way it will be a religious as well as an academic exercise for us and may well have practical consequences that reach far into the future.

A Question of Language

In the chapters that follow, I will be making frequent reference to the classical names for the three divine persons of the Christian doctrine of the Trinity: Father, Son, and Holy Spirit. Yet in the eyes of many contemporary Christians these same names or titles implicitly carry forward

---

[10] Ibid., 126–28.
[11] Ibid., 74–80.

and promote a form of patriarchy (literally, male authority) within Christianity, albeit unconsciously in most cases. Yet they remain the names most widely used both in public worship and in academic texts dealing with the doctrine of the Trinity. I thus face a modest dilemma in deciding how to deal with this issue. If I drop the classical names Father, Son, and Spirit and employ instead terms like Creator, Redeemer, and Sanctifier, I will surely please some readers. Yet there are problems in identifying each of the divine persons simply with a single role or function in salvation history. After all, all three persons should be involved in creation, redemption, and sanctification, albeit in different ways. But if I simply use the classical names without further qualification, I run the risk of offending still others. My solution in this book is to call attention at this point to the purely metaphorical character of these names. God has no gender. Therefore, addressing the divine persons as Father, Son, and Holy Spirit is purely a matter of convention. In another age the terms Mother, Daughter, and Divine Breath might just as readily have been used. Second, I will have a chapter later in the book devoted to the issue of gender and God language where I summarize and evaluate the arguments of several prominent feminists about the gender bias implicit in the customary use of male names and titles for the three divine persons. While not always agreeing with their theoretical conclusions and action proposals, I have learned from these feminists the importance of the language one uses in referring to God. For what is ultimately at stake in this matter is not simply the vindication of the rights of women within the church and society at large. The overthrow of patriarchy and what it stands for in terms of the alleged superiority of men over women by reason of natural law or divine decree is equally important for men, albeit in different ways than for women. The truth must ultimately prevail on this issue if the divine plan both for the human race and indeed for all of creation is to be realized. Given this caution in the use of God language, let us begin our historical overview of the Christian doctrine of God.

Part One

Retrieval of the Tradition

Chapter One

The Birth of a Revolutionary Belief

In today's world Judaism and Christianity are seen as separate religions with different practices and beliefs. Jews go to synagogue on Friday night and Saturday morning. Christians go to church on Saturday evening or Sunday morning. Within the tabernacle in a Jewish synagogue Jews keep handwritten scrolls of the Torah (the first five books of the Hebrew Bible). Within the tabernacle in their churches, many Christians keep the Holy Eucharist, consecrated hosts believed to be the ongoing physical presence of Jesus Christ, the risen Lord and Savior, in this world. Jews thus believe in divine revelation, above all, as found in the Torah, the written Word of God. Christians believe in divine revelation in the person of Jesus, the Incarnate Word of God. The life and teachings of Jesus, to be sure, are recorded in the gospel narratives; likewise, St. Paul and the other New Testament writers offer inspired commentary on the life and teaching of Jesus. But for Christians the primary source of divine revelation is not a text like the Torah but the person of Jesus Christ who is both divine and human. Much the same could be said about the differences between Christians and Muslims. Whereas Muslims treasure the Koran as the written Word of God dictated to Mohammed by God in the seventh century CE, Christians, as noted above, regard the New Testament as secondary to Jesus himself as the Incarnate Word of God.

God as One in the Hebrew Bible

Christians, Jews, and Muslims thus believe in God. But whereas Jews and Muslims believe that God is one person, Christians believe that God is three persons who are nevertheless together one God. How this paradoxical belief, that God is both one and three at the same time, came about needs further explanation. As the book of Genesis testifies, Abraham was the father of the Jewish nation, since he was called by God to leave his ancestral home in Haran (located in contemporary Iraq) and journey westward to the land of Canaan (modern day Israel/Palestine) and there to found a great nation (Gen 12:1-3). At the time of Abraham virtually every tribe had its own god to whom the tribe looked for survival in competition with other tribes and with the forces of nature. So it was not unusual that Abraham and his family should likewise worship a god to whom they looked for protection. But the temptation, if not for Abraham himself, at least for his descendants, was to change gods, to worship the gods of their neighbors if they saw any political or economic advantage in doing so. Thus worship of many gods rather than of the one God who spoke to Abraham and promised to make him the father of a great nation was an ongoing problem for the Israelites, the descendants of Abraham, throughout their long history.

There were, however, key moments in that history when the Israelites recognized that they must worship the God of their fathers, Abraham, Isaac, and Jacob, and not the gods of the people with whom they lived. One of those moments came during the exile of the Israelites in Egypt, the land to which they had migrated earlier because of a famine in their own land of Israel. The Israelites were at that point in time a captive people forced to do hard manual labor by the Egyptians. But, as recorded in the book of Exodus, God raised up a leader for the Israelites named Moses who would deliver his people from their captivity in Egypt and lead them back to their homeland. Early in that pilgrimage Moses received the Ten Commandments from God on Mount Sinai, the first of which was to worship God in exclusion of all other gods:

> I, the LORD, am your God, who brought you out of the land of Egypt, that place of slavery. You shall not have other gods besides me. You shall not carve idols for yourselves in the shape of anything in the sky above or on the earth below or in the waters beneath the earth; you shall not bow down before them or worship them. For I, the LORD, your God, am a jealous God, inflicting punishment for their fathers' wickedness on the children of those who hate me, down to the third and fourth generation; but bestowing mercy down to the thousandth generation, on the children of those who love me and keep my commandments. (Exod 20:2-6)

Still another dramatic moment in the history of God's dealing with the Israelites came in the time of King David (1000–962 BCE) and his son Solomon (961–922 BCE) when the first temple to Yahweh, the God of Israel, was erected. Previously the people of Israel felt the presence of Yahweh with the ark of the covenant, a portable tabernacle carried on poles by chosen Israelites as they moved from place to place in their long journey to the Promised Land (Canaan) and then kept in one place once they crossed the Jordan River and conquered the local inhabitants. But with King David's military victories and in the time of peace during the reign of his son Solomon, the Israelites built a permanent home for the ark of the covenant in the form of a large temple in Jerusalem, David's capital city. Some centuries later, in 587 BCE, this temple was destroyed by the Babylonians. But after their return from exile in Babylon, the Israelites rebuilt the temple, which lasted until after the time of Jesus and was eventually destroyed by the Romans in 70 CE as punishment for the rebellion of the Israelites against Roman occupation.

The New Christian Experience of God

This brief historical overview is only intended to make clear how important belief in one God was to the ancient Israelites. They had to struggle to continue worshiping Yahweh in the midst of their neighbors who practiced various forms of polytheism. Imagine the consternation of most inhabitants of Jerusalem and Palestine, therefore, when the early Christians proclaimed that Jesus was divine and was to be worshiped as God with the same status as his Father in heaven, Yahweh, the traditional God of Israel. Likewise, St. Paul's writings and the Gospel of John make repeated references to still a third divine personality, the Holy Spirit, who regularly descended upon newly baptized Christians giving them the gift of speaking in foreign languages, the gift of prophecy or interpretation of these strange languages, and other miraculous ("charismatic") gifts. For ordinary Jews this was yet another indication that the early Christians had abandoned their Jewish heritage, belief in one God, and become polytheists, worshipers of many gods, after the fashion of their pagan neighbors within the Roman Empire.

But for these early Christians who as faithful Jews still went to the synagogue or temple on a regular basis, there was no denying their personal and group experience, even if it posed theoretical problems for continued belief in one God. They all still worshiped Yahweh, the God of Israel, whom Jesus in his lifetime addressed with the familiar name

"Abba," Daddy. The apostles and other witnesses of the life of Jesus, however, testified that Jesus was more than human. He preached with uncommon authority and worked healing miracles during his public career. But above all, in the manner of his death and his appearances to his followers after his resurrection, his divinity shone through. Thomas's profession of faith, "My Lord and my God" (John 20:28), summed up the impact that Jesus as the risen Lord had on the majority of his followers. Finally, with the coming of the Holy Spirit to the disciples in the upper room at Pentecost (Acts 2:1-4) and in the Spirit's manifestation to the Jerusalem community at other times (e.g., Acts 4:31; 10:44-46), it was clear to them that, besides God the Father and his Son Jesus the Christ, there was a third divine personality at work in their lives. Deciding how to defend the reality of these three divine persons while at the same time retaining traditional belief in God as one, however, took several centuries for the early Christians to think through and eventually to formulate in articles of belief, initially the Apostles Creed (*Symbolum Apostolicum*) and then much later the Nicene-Constantinople Creed (recited in many churches every weekend after the homily).

Work of the Early Fathers of the Church

Johannes Quasten, in his monumental three-volume work titled *Patrology*, traces the development of the doctrine of the Trinity and other Christian beliefs over the first four hundred years of the Christian era. I will make brief reference to a few of the fathers of the church whose life and work he analyzes. Quasten notes, first of all, that a rudimentary form of the Apostles' Creed was in circulation almost from the time of the apostles, although its exact authorship remains unclear.[1] This early creed referring to the Father, the Son, and the Holy Spirit (Matt 28:19) was used in the ceremony of baptism when converts were immersed three times into the baptismal pool. Likewise, the early Christian writer Justin Martyr in the first of his *Apologies*, or Explanations of the Christian Faith to non-Christians, about the year 150 makes reference to baptism in the name of the three divine persons.

As Quasten further explains, however, Justin was not clear on the relationship between Jesus as the Word Incarnate and God the Father, Creator of heaven and earth. Justin compared Jesus as the Word Incarnate

---

[1] Johannes Quasten, *Patrology*, vol. 1 (Westminster, MD: Newman Press, 1960), 23–24.

with the *Logos* (Word), the principle of order and intelligibility within this world according to the philosophy of Stoicism. Hence, Jesus would seem to be less divine than the Father as the source of all that exists.[2] Another of the early church fathers, Athenagoras, clearly affirmed the equality of the Divine Word, or Second Person of the Trinity, with the Father. But neither he nor Justin had a clearly defined understanding of the third divine person, the Holy Spirit. Finally, Irenaeus, bishop of Lyons in France at the end of the second century, claimed that the divine Son and the Holy Spirit were the "two hands" of God the Father in the work of salvation as recorded in both the Hebrew Bible, or Old Testament, and the New Testament.[3] Furthermore, in opposition to some Gnostic teachings, Irenaeus made clear that there are not two gods, one good and one evil, at work in human history but only one and the same trinitarian God: Father, Son, and Holy Spirit.

But this was just the beginning of efforts to give a rational justification for Christian belief in God as Trinity. Clement of Alexandria in the third century, for example, deepened Justin Martyr's notion of Jesus as the Word Incarnate who is both creator of the world and the revelation of the Father to human beings. As the Logos or Word Incarnate, Jesus is "the saviour of the human race and the founder of a new life which begins with faith, proceeds to knowledge and contemplation and leads through love and charity to immortality and deification."[4] Clement's successor at Alexandria, Origen, was accused of heresy by many of his contemporaries, but his teaching on the Trinity still represented a major step forward in thinking through what is meant by the expression "three persons in one God."

Origen's Controversial Theories

Origen recognized that if God is pure spirit, the Son cannot originate from the Father by some sort of physical generation but only by an eternal spiritual generation.[5] So, contrary to what the celebrated heretic Arius would later claim, there never was a time when the divine Son did not exist. Father and Son were of one and the same spiritual substance, *homoousios*, as the Council of Nicaea would later affirm. At the same time,

[2] Ibid., 209.
[3] Ibid., 294–95.
[4] Quasten, *Patrology*, vol 2 (Westminster, MD: Newman Press, 1964), 22.
[5] Ibid., 78.

Origen claimed that only God the Father was unbegotten so that techni-cally the divine Son was a "second" God, and the Holy Spirit was even lower in rank within the Trinity than the Son: "we say that the Saviour and the Holy Spirit are without comparison and are very much superior to all things that are made, but also that the Father is even more above them than they are themselves above creatures even the highest."[6] Many theologians even today would say that this is heretical because it makes the Son and the Spirit less divine than the Father. Origin may have had in mind only a necessary hierarchical order among the divine persons. If so, he was presumably influenced by the teachings of the Neoplatonists, who believed that everything in this world emanates from an absolutely transcendent deity, the One, and eventually through various intermedi-aries returns to it.[7] In any case, Origen was clearly influenced by the Platonists in his belief that the souls of human beings existed in a purely spiritual realm prior to their existence in a physical body within this world.[8] Life in this world was thus both a punishment for sin committed in the prior realm of the spirit and an opportunity for redemption and return to full union with God.

Tertullian and Other Western Theologians

Meanwhile, elsewhere in the early Christian world, a somewhat dif-ferent approach to the Trinity gradually took shape. Whereas Origen and other theologians in the Eastern Mediterranean tended to be guilty of subordinationism in dealing with the doctrine of the Trinity, that is, in treating the Son and Holy Spirit as subordinate in status to the Father, Western theologians like Tertullian subtly moved in the direction of modalism, one God in three distinct "modes" or ways of existing. Writing against the heretic Praxeas who claimed that the Father rather than the Son became incarnate as Jesus, Tertullian stressed the divine monarchy shared equally by all three divine persons:

> Three, however, not in quality, but in sequence, not in substance,
> but in form, not in power but in aspect; yet of one substance and
> one quality and one power, because there is one God from whom

[6] Ibid., 79. Reference is to Origen's commentary on John's gospel, 13:25: "the Father is greater than I" (John 14:28).

[7] J. N. D. Kelly, *Early Christian Doctrines*, 2nd ed. (New York: Harper & Row, 1960), 131–32.

[8] Ibid., 131; also Quasten, *Patrology*, vol. 2, 91–92.

these sequences and forms and aspects are reckoned out in the name of the Father and the Son and the Holy Spirit.[9]

Tertullian in North Africa and his contemporary Hippolytus in Rome both made use of Irenaeus's notion of the "economy" of salvation, the way in which the three divine persons functioned within human history as recorded in the Bible. Thus they tended to distinguish between the Divine Word within the Trinity and the divine Son who became incarnate in Jesus. But Son and Holy Spirit are both "persons" and God is a "Trinity," according to Tertullian, thus coining the term that would later be used at the Council of Nicaea and afterward.[10] Yet the tendency to modalism remained in that the word "person" in Latin originally meant "mask," a device for projecting one's voice in theater productions.[11] Are then the persons of the Trinity just masks for one and the same God behind the masks?

Two other theologians with strong modalist tendencies, who subsequently were declared heretics because of their views, were Paul of Samosata and Sabellius. Though they differed in their approaches to the monarchy or rule of God in this world, they both ended up as virtual unitarians (believers in one God), not trinitarians (believers in the Trinity). Paul of Samosata proposed that Christ was a human being inspired by divine Wisdom. Hence, while he continued to refer to the Trinity, what he really meant was that "the Son and the Spirit were merely the Church's names for the inspired man Jesus Christ and the grace which God poured upon the apostles."[12] Equivalently, then, Jesus was Son of God by adoption at his baptism by John the Baptist rather than by nature from all eternity. Sabellius proposed that the one God took different forms in dealing with human beings: "Thus the one Godhead regarded as creator and law-giver was Father; for redemption It was projected like a ray of the sun and was then withdrawn; then, thirdly, the same Godhead operated as Spirit to inspire and bestow grace."[13] Sabellius's notion of God, accordingly, was quite impersonal. Not a personal God, but the Godhead (the nature of God) took on three different forms in dealing with human beings.

---

[9] Quasten, *Patrology*, vol. 2, 286; see also Kelly, *Early Christian Doctrines*, 110–15.
[10] Kelly, *Early Christian Doctrines*, 112–13.
[11] Ibid., 115.
[12] Ibid., 118.
[13] Ibid., 122.

One more theologian out of the Western Mediterranean world should be mentioned before moving to the dramatic events that took place at the beginning of the fourth century. Novatian was a third-century Roman theologian who wrote a treatise on the Trinity that advanced the trinitarian theology of Tertullian and Hippolytus by urging that the Divine Word, or Second Person of the Trinity, was Son of God, not just in the economy of salvation within this world, but from all eternity: "He Who is born before all time must be said to have always existed in the Father; for a date in time cannot be fixed for Him Who is before all time. He is eternally in the Father; otherwise the Father were not always Father."[14] Yet Novatian himself could be accused of a subtle subordinationism in his treatment of the relations between Father and Son within the Trinity. Referring to New Testament texts in which Christ speaks of himself as coming forth from the Father and returning to the Father, Novatian sometimes speaks of Christ as the Father's "messenger" or "angel."[15]

Arius and Arianism

All of these theological speculations about Christian belief in the Trinity came to a head at the beginning of the fourth century in the person of Arius, a priest of Alexandria in Egypt who contended that Christ was not divine but only the first creature of God. After all, if God is unbegotten and therefore strictly immutable, then God cannot share the divine being without undergoing change: "Therefore whatever else exists must have come into existence, not by any communication of God's being, but by an act of creation on His part, i.e., must have been called into existence out of nothing."[16] Moreover, did not St. Paul in his epistle to the Colossians (1:15) refer to Christ as "the firstborn of all creation"? Hence, Christ, the Divine Word, must be a creature who serves as the mediator between God as completely transcendent to the world and the world of creation. To be sure, Christ "is a perfect creature, and not to be compared with the rest of creation; but that He is a creature, owing His being wholly to the Father's will, follows from the primary fact that He is not self-existent."[17] As a creature of God the Father, therefore, Christ had a beginning.

---

[14] Quasten, *Patrology*, vol. 2, 227. Reference is to Novatian's *De Trinitate*, 31.

[15] Quasten, *Patrology*, vol. 2, 228–29; see also Gerard S. Sloyan, *The Three Persons in One God* (Englewood Cliffs, NJ: Prentice-Hall, 1964), 45.

[16] Kelly, *Early Christian Doctrines*, 227.

[17] Ibid., 228.

Although born outside of time, prior to his generation by the Father he did not exist: "There was when He was not."[18] Christ being called the Son of God is simply a metaphor to express his exalted dignity as God's first creature.

In many ways, Arius and his followers were simply drawing out the logical consequences of the subordinationism implicit in the teaching of Origen. But whereas Origen had distinguished between the Father first begetting the Son from all eternity and later creating the physical world, Arius saw these actions of the Father as being basically one and the same. On a deeper level, however, what was subtly at work here was a distrust of change or alteration wherever it happens. Whatever is subject to change is by that very fact imperfect. What is perfect does not change since by change is normally meant a falling away from an original perfection. There was apparently among the ancients little or no expectation that from change could come further perfection, hence, that change could be for the better rather than for the worse. Furthermore, as Ivor Leclerc pointed out some years ago, this distinction between God as perfect and immutable and the world of creation as imperfect and subject to change is still alive today in the minds of many Christians, having been carried over from the ancient world first into the medieval period and then into the modern era.[19]

The Council of Nicaea

In any event, noting the considerable unease among bishops and even lay people in the church of the Eastern Mediterranean, Emperor Constantine convened in 325 an ecumenical council of bishops at Nicaea, in modern-day Turkey, so as to secure doctrinal orthodoxy on the matter and restore calm to the empire. More than three hundred bishops participated and drew up the Nicene Creed, which reaffirms that Jesus Christ is divine, the only Son of God, begotten not made, of one substance with the Father.[20] What remained unclear in the term "of the same substance," however, was whether or not the Father and the Son shared numerically one and the same divine substance or whether they shared generically the same divine substance (just as two human beings share generically

---

[18] Ibid.

[19] Ivor Leclerc, *The Nature of Physical Existence* (New York: Humanities Press, 1972), 59–69.

[20] Kelly, *Early Christian Doctrines*, 231–37.

the same human nature). All that was really clear was that there was no physical division of the divine substance between the Father and the Son because that would mean change or alteration in the nature of God. Emperor Constantine had achieved peace within the empire but only at the price of an ambiguous definition of the divinity of Christ, which was immediately interpreted differently by different groups within the church.

As Gerard Sloyan points out, Arius's sympathizers did not give up easily.[21] The expression *homoousios* was not to be found in Scripture. Can strictly philosophical non-Scriptural terms be used to clarify Christian belief? Furthermore, even from a philosophical perspective, Arius's position was simpler and easier to understand. By definition God is self-sufficient and autonomous. Why then does God need the Son and the Spirit in order to be God? Behind this complaint, of course, was the assumption that human as well as divine perfection consisted in being or becoming self-sufficient, not depending on others to achieve one's goals in life. The alternate ideal of relationality and intersubjectivity, harmonious existence in community with others as the goal of human striving, was apparently not much in vogue at that time.

Semi-Arianism

In due time, the term *homoousios*, of the same substance, was replaced in the minds of many bishops and lay people with a new term, *homoiousios*, of like substance. Thus was born what has been called Semi-Arianism. Saint Cyril of Jerusalem used *homoiousios* to speak of the Father and the Son as Two who are both God because they have the same will and operation. Others, however, used the new term in a more strictly Arian sense to indicate that the Son was indeed a creature but bore a moral resemblance to the Father.[22] Saint Athanasius, who was secretary to the bishop of Alexandria at the Council of Nicaea and who later became bishop of that see himself, became the chief advocate for retention of the term *homoousios* to avoid all ambiguity about the divinity of Christ. He argued that, if the Son is like the Father in all things, then the Son is also like the Father in substance or essence and thus equally divine with the Father.

---

[21] Sloyan, *The Three Persons in One God*, 62–65.
[22] Ibid., 64.

Similarly, Hilary of Poitiers (in southern France) urged in *On the Trinity* that the term *homoiousios* was just as unscriptural as *homoousios*. So why not use *homoouosios* rather than *homoiousios* to make clear that one is not secretly an Arian, one who thinks of Christ as the creature of the Father?[23] Ironically, both Athanasius and Hilary were persecuted and exiled from their dioceses for their efforts to defend the divinity of Christ. Yet, inasmuch as in their time of exile they lived in different parts of the Mediterranean world (Athanasius in Rome, Hilary in Asia Minor), they learned from their enforced exile the different thought patterns of Christians in the Western and Eastern Mediterranean. Thus they were better able afterward to offer a suitable compromise position that bridged these linguistic differences and kept the church of one mind about the divinity of Christ.

The Divinity of the Holy Spirit

Eventually the focus of attention for Christians of the fourth century shifted from Christ to the Spirit. The Arians, of course, claimed that the Spirit was as different from the Son as the Son was different in substance from the Father. But even orthodox believers were unsure how to describe the status of the Spirit within the life of the Trinity. Was the Spirit perhaps a second Son of the Father or only a personification of the common spirit or mind-set between the Father and the Son? The Nicene Creed had simply affirmed the divinity of the Spirit without further qualification. What was needed was further theological reflection on the relations between the divine persons and an expanded definition of the work of the Spirit in salvation history, which eventually came at the First Council of Constantinople in 381.

As might be expected, Athanasius was just as staunch in his defense of the divinity of the Holy Spirit as in his defense of the divinity of the Son: "Athanasius argues from effect to cause: since the Spirit makes us holy with the holiness of God by dwelling in us as in a temple (1 Cor 3:16ff.), he must be divine. He therefore shares one and the same substance with the Father and Son."[24] Athanasius likewise describes the joint activity of the Father, Son, and Holy Spirit in creation and the work of redemption as follows: the Father accomplishes all things through the Word in the Holy Spirit. As we will see in chapter 2, this became the canonized phrase

[23] Ibid., 66.
[24] Ibid., 68.

for the Eastern Orthodox churches in their struggle with the church in the West over the way in which the Holy Spirit proceeded from the Father and the Son. But at the time not everyone agreed with Athanasius and Cyril of Jerusalem in their strong defense of the divinity of the Holy Spirit. A group of Christians called the Macedonians or Pneumatomachians ("Spirit-fighters") challenged the divinity of the Spirit but were rebuffed, first by more orthodox theologians and then by the decrees of the Council of Constantinople. Chief among those orthodox theologians were the Cappadocian Fathers: Saints Basil the Great, Gregory of Nyssa, and Gregory of Nazianz. We will take up their important contribution to the standard Eastern Orthodox doctrine of the Trinity in the next chapter.

Conclusion

We can bring to a close this first chapter on the development of the doctrine of the Trinity by noting how important theology was to the lives of the early Christians. Bishops, theologians, and even ordinary people engaged in intense debate about the divinity of Christ and the Holy Spirit. Whether in cafes over something to drink or at the marketplace in search of food for dinner, Christians got into heated arguments over theological issues. As noted above, Emperor Constantine personally called the Council of Nicaea so as to settle these theological issues, given their strong political overtones that threatened the peace and harmony of the empire. Likewise, in the medieval and early modern periods of Western history, religion and politics were closely aligned. Only in recent centuries here in the West has religion become largely a private affair, not to be discussed except occasionally with close friends. There are political advantages, to be sure, in separating church and state, as in the United States at present. But there are also disadvantages in the ways in which we sometimes fail to give witness to our deepest convictions. In any event, the controversies over the doctrine of the Trinity in the first four centuries of the church's existence are among the most colorful in its long history. Moreover, as we shall see in the course of this book, most of the basic positions that one can assume with respect to the doctrine of the Trinity were already in place by the end of the fourth century: subordinationism or implicit tritheism, on the one hand; modalism or adoptionism, on the other hand.

Chapter Two

The Standoff between East and West in Medieval Christianity

After the Council of Constantinople in 381, the focus of debate among bishops, theologians, and interested laypeople within the ancient Christian world shifted from the doctrine of the Trinity to the person of Christ. If Christ was truly divine as well as human, as the Councils of Nicaea and Constantinople had defined, how is one to understand that dynamic union of divinity and humanity within the person of Christ so that neither is absorbed into the other? The Council at Ephesus in 431 and the Council of Chalcedon in 451 dealt with these issues. Two different christologies or theoretical approaches to the person of Christ were involved: the one focusing on the divinity of Christ and promoted by Cyril of Alexandria, and the other focusing on the humanity of Christ and set forth by Nestorius, bishop of Constantinople. But how the fathers of the church resolved this question is the work of another volume in this series.[1] I mention it here only to make clear that the theological ferment generated by intense debate over the doctrine of the Trinity did not die out with the Council of Constantinople but simply shifted direction and focus. Theology was still a hot topic of conversation among educated people for many years to come.

In this chapter I will sketch how the doctrine of the Trinity underwent further development in the centuries after the Council of Constantinople,

---

[1] See Gerard S. Sloyan, *Jesus: Word Made Flesh*, Engaging Theology: Catholic Perspectives (Collegeville, MN: Liturgical Press, 2008).

following one line of thought in the Western Mediterranean and still another line of thought in the Eastern Mediterranean. As we shall see later in the chapter, this divergence in the interpretation of the decrees of Nicaea and Constantinople eventually led to the Great Schism in 1054 when the delegates of Pope Leo IX excommunicated the patriarch of Constantinople and were themselves then condemned by a synod of Eastern bishops in Constantinople. Naturally, other more mundane factors also played a role in this standoff between East and West: rivalry between the pope in Rome and the patriarch of Constantinople, the use of different languages (Latin and Greek) in the liturgy and official documents, uneasy relations between East and West in dealing with the threat of Islam in the Mediterranean world. Likewise, the "Councils of Reunion" —at Lyons, France, in 1274 and Florence, Italy, in 1439—did not bring about an enduring reconciliation between the leaders of the church in the West and in the East. Only in the recent pontificate of John Paul II were steps taken toward reconciliation of the churches with one another, but even here no one was talking about full reunion.

Augustine's Theology of the Trinity

So different beliefs do make a difference in practical church life and discipline. Keeping this in mind, we will sketch how the doctrine of the Trinity developed differently in the West and in the East. Perhaps the most notable trinitarian theologian in the West prior to the High Middle Ages (thirteenth century) was Augustine, bishop of Hippo (354–430). In his lengthy treatise on the Trinity composed over twenty years' time, Augustine set the pattern for Western understanding of the doctrine of the Trinity. He primarily focused on the nature of God (what makes God to be one) rather than on the differences among the divine persons: "Even though it is not the same thing to be the Father and to be the Son, nevertheless the substance is not different because these designations do not belong to the order of substance but of relation; a relation which is not accidental because it is not mutable."[2] So Father, Son, and Holy Spirit have different relations to one another as distinct persons but have one and the same substance, or divine being. In their dynamic interrelation

---

[2] Angelo Di Berardino, ed., and Placid Solari, OSB, trans., *Patrology* (Westminster, MD: Christian Classics, 1988), 428. Reference is to St. Augustine, *The Trinity*, trans. Stephen McKenna (Washington, DC: Catholic University of America Press, 1963), Bk. 5, chap. 5, n. 6.

they are like the human soul with its three interdependent functions (memory, understanding, and will), but unlike the human soul each of these functions is a different person who possesses the divine nature in a different way than the other two persons.[3]

In this way Augustine excluded the possibility of subordinationism within the Trinity. The Son and the Spirit are equally God with the Father even though the Father is the "origin" of the Trinity in that he generates the Son and empowers the Son to breathe forth the Spirit in the Son's response to the Father.[4] The Spirit is accordingly not a second Son of the Father but the gift of divine love between the Father and the Son. There is, therefore, a major difference between the generation of the Son from the Father and the procession of the Spirit from the relationship of the Father and the Son to one another.[5] As we will see below, this "psychological" model for the doctrine of the Trinity had a great influence on Thomas Aquinas in his own formulation of the trinitarian mystery. At the same time, this approach to the doctrine of the Trinity was notably different from that developed in the Eastern church by the Cappadocian Fathers and their successors, as we shall see later. Theologians in the Eastern church presumed the differences between the divine persons and sought to prove how God, though three distinct persons, is still one. Augustine and Aquinas thought instead that God must be one, and then explained how this one divine life or way of existing could be shared perfectly by three different persons.

Between Augustine and Thomas Aquinas

Intermediate between Augustine and Aquinas, however, were a number of distinguished Western theologians, of whom we will mention only a few. Boethius was a sixth-century Christian philosopher perhaps best known for *The Consolation of Philosophy*, which he wrote in prison while awaiting execution. Therein he "consoled" himself about his upcoming death with the thought that even in their misfortunes good people are by reason of their virtuous lives happier than bad people.[6] But in still another work Boethius formulated a definition of personhood that would have a major impact on the subsequent development of the doctrine of

---

[3] Ibid., 429. Reference is to *The Trinity*, Bk. 15, chap. 3, n. 5.

[4] Ibid., 428. Reference is to *The Trinity*, Bk. 15, chap. 17, n. 29.

[5] Ibid., 429. Reference is to *The Trinity*, Bk. 15, chap. 27, n. 50.

[6] Boethius, *The Consolation of Philosophy*, trans. Joel C. Relihan (Indianapolis, IN: Hackett, 2001).

the Trinity in the West. In his view, a person is an individual who is rational by nature, able to think and make conscious decisions. This fits human beings quite nicely; but applied to the divine persons without qualification, this seems to imply belief in three gods, all of them rational individuals, instead of one God in three persons. This misunderstanding of what it means to be a person was eventually cleared up in the twelfth century by Richard of St. Victor.[7] Father, Son, and Holy Spirit are three persons and yet one God because each is the reality of God in a totally different way that cannot be shared with the other two. Only one of them can be Father, only one can be Son, and only one can be Spirit. Yet all three are needed to be the full reality of God. The persons of the Trinity have paradoxically everything in common except their differences, as Anselm of Canterbury had already pointed out.[8] Since being Father and being Son are logically opposed to one another, the Father and the Son must be different persons but living the same divine life. Similarly, since the Holy Spirit is the one who is breathed forth by the Father and the Son together, the Spirit is different from both of them and thus still a third person within the triune God.

One more significant influence on Aquinas's approach to the Trinity was the Fourth Lateran Council held in Rome in 1215. At that ecumenical council, the church fathers rejected the teaching of Abbot Joachim of Flora, a Cistercian monk, on the doctrine of the Trinity. Joachim believed that God was in fact a quaternity, not a trinity: namely, three persons and their common nature. But the church fathers responded as follows:

> We believe and confess . . . that there is one supreme reality—incomprehensible, ineffable—which is in truth Father, Son, and Holy Spirit; three persons, both simultaneously and taken singly: therefore in God there is trinity only, not quaternity; for what is proper to the three persons is that reality (*res*) which is substance, essence, or divine nature. This is the principle of all else; no other can be found.[9]

Just how one and the same divine nature can be at work enabling the Father to beget the Son, the Son to be begotten, the Father and the Son to breathe forth the Spirit, and the Spirit to be breathed forth was not further

---

[7] Sloyan, *The Three Persons in One God*, 87. Reference is to Richard of St. Victor, *On the Trinity*, 4/22.

[8] Ibid., 84. Reference is to St. Anselm's *On the Procession of the Holy Spirit*, 7.

[9] Ibid., 89. Reference is to *Enchiridion Symbolorum, Definitionum et Declarationum de Rebus Fidei et Morum* (Freiburg in Breisgau, Germany: Herder & Herder, 1964), n. 804.

explained by this definition. Even so, it set the ground rules for the way in which Aquinas would think about the Trinity a generation later.

Abbot Joachim was also noted for one other heresy regarding the Trinity, a heresy that in one way or another has lasted over the centuries even into the twenty-first century. Joachim thought that the history of the human race could be divided into different ages, with one of the divine persons presiding over each age. The history of the human race up to the time of Jesus was the Age of the Father. From the time of Jesus until now the human race has existed in the Age of the Son. But the Age of the Spirit is fast approaching, when lay people as well as monks and nuns will live like free spirits, simply following the internal inspiration of the Holy Spirit. Because of its implicit threat to the established institutional structure of the church, this "spiritualist" movement was condemned by the church fathers at the Fourth Lateran Council in 1215. But the idea of successive ages of the world dominated by different divine persons has persisted in the minds of reformers and revolutionaries both inside and outside the church. The boast of Nazis, for example, about the coming of the Third Reich in Germany in the 1930s is clearly a secularized version of the theology of Joachim. Likewise, New Age thinking, belief in the forthcoming Age of Aquarius, in the 1960s may also be traced to the same hope for the Age of the Spirit in which human beings will at last live as free spirits.

Aquinas on the Trinity

Turning now to Aquinas's doctrine of the Trinity, we note first how he mentally played around with the notion of procession.[10] Processions, he says, are both external and internal. External processions take place when two separate entities relate to one another as cause and effect. Internal processions, on the contrary, exist within a single entity, as in the "procession" of a thought or idea from the mind of a human being. The procession of the Divine Word from the mind of the Father is thus an internal procession within the divine life. Likewise, the procession of the Holy Spirit from the joint action of the Father and the Son is an internal procession within the divine life, somewhat like the way in which we human beings internally cherish someone we love in our minds and

---

[10] S.Thomae Aquinatis, *Summa Theologiae* (Madrid: Biblioteca de Autores Cristianos, 1951), part 1, question 27, art. 1.

hearts.[11] Moreover, says Aquinas, there can only be two such internal processions within God because, like us, God has both mind and will on which the processions of the Son and of the Spirit are based but nothing else from which still another internal procession could come.[12] Aquinas evidently follows the lead of Augustine here in making an analogy between ourselves and God. Like us, God possesses mind and will. But in God's case mind and will are the bases for the existence of three distinct persons within God, rather than simply two faculties or mental functions within one person. Like Augustine, therefore, Aquinas avoids the heresy of subordinationism among the divine persons but seems to be uncomfortably close to the opposite heresy of modalism. For to a skeptic the Father would seem to be the original Self within God who first becomes the Son through his knowledge of himself and then becomes the Spirit through his love for himself. Aquinas would counterargue, of course, that the analogy between ourselves and God is extremely limited.[13] This is certainly true, but it still exposes a problem within the classical Western approach to the doctrine of the Trinity.

This problem might have been resolved if Aquinas had thought through more carefully something else that he held in common with Augustine and Anselm about the doctrine of the Trinity, namely, that the three divine persons are "subsistent relations": their relations to one another constitute their very being and coexistence.[14] We human beings, for example, have relations of various kinds with different people, but none of them are identical with our very being or way of life. We owe our parents the origin of our existence in this world. But once born we have our own existence and activity as independent human beings, above all as we grow to maturity in adulthood. Hence, all our human relations are accidental or contingent insofar as they do not strictly define who we are as human beings. But the Father is nothing else but Fatherhood; that is what it means for him to be God. The Son, in turn, is nothing else but Sonhood. He can never be anything else but the Son within the divine life. The Holy Spirit, finally, is defined in his personhood as the only one of the divine persons who can be breathed forth by the Father and the Son. Thus being Father, being Son, and being Spirit are three coequal ways of being God since none of them can exist apart from the other two. Each one needs the other two to be himself in his very being. As mentioned

---

[11] Ibid., art. 3.
[12] Ibid., art. 5.
[13] Ibid., question 32, art. 1.
[14] Ibid., question 29, art. 4.

earlier, Anselm said that the three divine persons have everything in common except their different relations to one another. Thus what on the one hand binds them to one another (their necessary relations to one another) is on the other hand the basis for their differences from one another.

The brilliance of this insight into the simultaneous unity and diversity among the divine persons, however, should not blind us to the fact that it is still more a triumph of speculative logic than anything else. It has, in other words, little or no carryover value for the relations of human persons either to God or to one another in this world. This is probably the single biggest reason why the doctrine of the Trinity as thus elaborated by Augustine, Anselm, and Aquinas had relatively little impact on the spiritual life of Christians over the centuries until the present time. As we shall see in chapter 4, Karl Rahner, in beginning his book on the doctrine of the Trinity, lamented that contemporary Christians are practicing monotheists, with only lip service paid to the reality of the Trinity in their spiritual lives.[15]

A Fresh Look at the Doctrine

Two medieval theologians, however, were perhaps more down to earth in their reflections on the doctrine of the Trinity: Richard of St. Victor, mentioned above, and St. Bonaventure, a Franciscan contemporary of Aquinas in the thirteenth century. Richard of St. Victor came up with perhaps the first "social" model for the Trinity. Taking his cue partly from the medieval tradition of romantic love and partly from still another of Augustine's analogies for the Trinity in everyday life,[16] Richard suggested that if "God is love" (1 John 4:16), then God cannot be engaged simply in self-love or even in love for one other person. Rather, the perfection of love is shared love involving three persons in which each takes delight in the love of the other two for one another, quite apart from himself or herself: "Shared love is properly said to exist when a third person is loved by two persons harmoniously and in community, and the affection for the two persons is fused into one affection by the flame of love for the third."[17] Admittedly, this completely unselfish love for

---

[15] See below, chap. 4; likewise Karl Rahner, *The Trinity*, trans. Joseph Donceel (New York: Herder and Herder, 1970), 10.

[16] See Denis Edwards, *Jesus the Wisdom of God: An Ecological Theology* (Maryknoll, NY: Orbis, 1995), 91–110.

[17] Ibid., 97. Reference is to Richard of St. Victor, *On the Trinity*, 3/19.

others is to be found fully expressed only in God. But even as a humanly unattainable ideal, it nevertheless appeals strongly to us, both in our personal friendships and in our community with others, above all, in our understanding of the church as a community of friends in the Lord. The only question, of course, is whether this approach to the Trinity is tritheistic, implicitly claiming that there are three gods, not one God in three persons. Richard's answer to this objection was fairly conventional, namely, that they all share equally the very same substance or divine nature.[18] Together they are one reality, not three realities. As we will see in chapter 6, something more is needed by way of explanation in order to set aside the accusation of tritheism.

The second down to earth thinker was St. Bonaventure, who started with the notion of God as Supreme Goodness rather than Perfect Love. We all know, argued Bonaventure, that goodness is contagious; one good deed inspires another. So if God is Supreme Goodness, then God must have a very strong urge to create a world filled with divine goodness. Yet even before the creation of the world, there must be a "spilling-over" of goodness within God so as to bring about the eternal generation of the Son from the Father and the procession of the Holy Spirit from the love of the Father and the Son for one another.[19] The Father, accordingly, is the "Fountain of Goodness" (*fontalis plenitudo*) within God. All three divine persons are needed to be Supreme Goodness, but the Father enjoys a priority as the source of that same goodness. As we shall see momentarily, Bonaventure's thinking on the Trinity is thus closer to the mind-set of the Eastern church on the relation of the divine persons to one another than to the trinitarian theology of Augustine, Anselm, and Aquinas. Likewise, better than Augustine, Anselm, and Aquinas, Bonaventure lays stress on the basic goodness of creation and its participation in the divine life.

The Cappadocian Fathers in the Eastern Church

Now, however, it is time to review the development of the doctrine of the Trinity in the Eastern church and to see how differences in approach to the mystery of the Trinity eventually produced a split between Eastern

---

[18] Ibid., 98–99.

[19] Ibid., 102–4. See also Zachary Hayes, OFM, in his introduction to *Saint Bonaventure's Disputed Questions on the Mystery of the Trinity*, trans. Zachary Hayes (St. Bonaventure, NY: Franciscan Institute, 1979), 32–36.

and Western Christianity, a split that has endured to this day. We will begin with the Cappadocian Fathers (from Cappadocia in modern day Turkey), Basil, Gregory of Nyssa, and Gregory Nazianz, who were active already in the fourth century but whose influence on trinitarian thought in the East had a lasting influence. As J. N. D. Kelly notes, the common starting point for all of them in their reflection on the doctrine of the Trinity was the three divine persons, not the one divine nature or essence as in the West.[20] In part, this was due to the fact that they were consciously seeking to meet the objections of well-intentioned Semi-Arians who objected to the heresy of Arius (see chap. 1) but still had trouble thinking of three divine persons who are together only one God, a single undivided reality. Why not three persons who are just similar to one another in their common possession of divinity (like three human beings possessing the same human nature in different ways)? The three Cappadocians, however, insisted that this would result in tritheism, belief in three gods, not one God. Rather, one must remain faithful to the teaching of the council fathers at Nicaea and Constantinople, affirming that the Father, the Son, and the Holy Spirit are numerically one and the same God even as in their internal relations to one another and in their external activity vis-à-vis their creatures they are different.[21]

Admittedly, their way of explaining this belief was at times somewhat ambiguous. To his great credit, Basil succeeded in defining the difference between *ousia* (the Greek word for nature, or principle of activity) and *hypostasis* (the Greek word for person). In God there is only one *ousia* but three *hypostases*.[22] But Basil then confused the issue all over again by proposing that *ousia* represents what is universal and *hypostasis* what is particular within God.[23] This, however, leaves open the question whether the universal within God is abstract (i.e., divinity, like humanity in human beings) or concrete (God as a single undivided reality). If the former is the case, then Basil is a Semi-Arian without knowing it; if the latter, Basil is still faithful to the church teaching at Nicaea and Constantinople. As Quasten points out, Gregory of Nyssa likewise had difficulty in distinguishing between what is universal within God and what is particular or individual to each divine person. In the end, Gregory of Nyssa endorsed an extreme realism with reference to universal forms

---

[20] Kelly, *Early Christian Doctrines*, 264.

[21] Ibid., 267–68.

[22] Johannes Quasten, *Patrology*, vol. 3 (Utrecht: Spectrum, 1966), 228.

[23] Kelly, *Early Christian Doctrines*, 265.

or ideas: "Peter, Paul and Barnabas should be called one man not three men" since like the persons of the Trinity they share a common humanity.[24] Finally, while Gregory of Nazianz coined the term "procession" as the way in which the Spirit proceeds from the Father through the Son,[25] he was not clear on what the term meant: how, in other words, "procession" differs from "generation" in any realistic sense.[26]

The great merit of the Cappadocian Fathers, however, was that they grasped that the unity of the divine persons lies in their joint activity, first with respect to one another and then in dealing with their creatures. The divine nature, in other words, is a dynamic, not a static reality. Admittedly, we human beings experience the activity of the divine persons only with respect to ourselves. But it is easy to believe that their activity vis-à-vis their creatures reflects their own inner unity as one God. "If we observe a single activity of Father, Son and Holy Spirit, in no respect different in the case of any, we are obliged to infer unity of nature from the identity of activity; for Father, Son and Holy Spirit cooperate in sanctifying, quickening, consoling and so on."[27] This line of thought will eventually lead theologians in the Eastern church to the notion of *perichoresis* (mutual indwelling of the divine persons). In this way the divine persons mutually influence one another's being and activity by reason of these same internal relations to one another. As Alfred North Whitehead comments in *Adventures of Ideas*, this was potentially a major new philosophical insight into the way that everything in this world is interconnected and interdependent in imitation of the persons of the Trinity in dealing with one another. But, unhappily, the idea of *perichoresis* was never carried over from the doctrine of the Trinity to the world of creation.[28]

God as Mystery for John of Damascus and Gregory Palamas

Two more theologians of the Eastern church should be considered before taking up how the Eastern and Western churches separated over their different understandings of the doctrine of the Trinity. The first is St. John of Damascus, a sixth-century theologian who extensively used

---

[24] Quasten, *Patrology*, vol. 3, 286.

[25] Ibid., 250.

[26] Kelly, *Early Christian Doctrines*, 265.

[27] Ibid., 266.

[28] Alfred North Whitehead, *Adventures of Ideas* (New York: Free Press, 1967), 168–69.

the notion of *perichoresis* in his writings on the Trinity. As G. L. Prestige points out, the idea of the mutual indwelling of the divine persons originated with Athanasius and the Cappadocian Fathers in the fourth century.[29] But the term *perichoresis* came into usage much later. Whereas it had first been employed to describe the dynamic relation of the divine and human natures in Jesus, John of Damascus used it to describe the relation of the divine persons to one another within the divine being (*ousia*): "we do not call the Father and the Son and the Holy Ghost three Gods, but one God, the Holy Trinity. . . . For they are united, as we said, so as not to be confused, but to adhere closely together, and they have their circumincession [*perichoresis*] one in the other without any blending or mingling and without change or division in substance such as is the division held by Arius."[30] John of Damascus thereby avoided both modalism (one God under three forms or appearances), as advocated by Sabellius, and the subordination of the Son and the Spirit to the Father, as maintained by Arius.

John of Damascus also declared his belief in the ineffability and incomprehensibility of God as divine mystery.[31] Here he anticipated the work of Gregory Palamas, a fourteenth-century Eastern theologian who enjoys roughly the same reputation in the Eastern church as Aquinas does in the West. Gregory distinguished between the unknowable and incommunicable divine essence and divine uncreated energies in which creatures, above all human beings, can share. As Catherine Mowry LaCugna comments: "[t]he divine essence is fully present to the creature through the divine energies which are in some sense distinct but not separate from the divine essence."[32] Thus there are three different dimensions or levels of reality within the divine being, according to Palamas: "(i) the permanently unnameable and imparticipable divine essence; (ii) the uncreated energies; (iii) the three divine *hypostases*, Father, Son, Spirit."[33] Gregory's intent was to make clear how human beings could share in the divine life through participating in the divine energies and yet be separate from God in God's very being (*ousia*). But, says LaCugna, the long-term effect of this line of thought was to drive a wedge between

[29] G. L. Prestige, *God in Patristic Thought* (London: S.P.C.K., 1964), 284.

[30] Ibid., 294–98. See also St. John of Damascus, *The Orthodox Faith*, Bk. 1, chap. 8, in *Writings*, trans. Frederic H. Chase, Jr. (New York: Fathers of the Church, Inc., 1958), 187.

[31] John of Damascus, *The Orthodox Faith*, Bk. 1, chap. 1, in Writings, 165.

[32] Catherine Mowry LaCugna, *God For Us: The Trinity and Christian Life* (San Francisco: HarperCollins, 1991), 184.

[33] Ibid.

the inner life of God and the workings of God in salvation history: "By locating the divine persons in the inaccessible, imparticipable divine essence, Gregory in effect has removed the Trinity from our salvation."[34] In a later chapter, we will return to LaCugna's analysis of the doctrine of the Trinity in both East and West and determine whether or not her own position may be a bit overstated. But it seems in any event clear that Gregory logically separated what in fact is undivided within God. As the Cappadocian Fathers made clear, the divine persons do not *have* a divine nature (*ousia*); each of them *is* the divine nature, the full reality of God in a different way.

The Breakup of East and West over the Procession of the Spirit

How then did the split between the Eastern church and the Western church come about? From our perspective centuries later, it seems incredible that so much could have been made out of so little. But this is to forget how important the doctrine of the Trinity was to church leaders in the East and West at that time. Because they began their explanation of the doctrine of the Trinity with the one divine nature or essence primarily in mind, Western theologians like Augustine (and later Aquinas) claimed that the Holy Spirit proceeds both *from* the Father and *from* the Son as they together breathe forth the Holy Spirit. Eastern theologians, on the contrary, with their starting point for explanation of the Trinity in the plurality of the divine persons and in their belief that the Father is the source of the divine life for all three persons, instead affirmed that the Spirit proceeds from the Father alone but *through* the mediation of the Son. This may seem a trivial distinction to us, but it also had important political implications, above all for the church in the East. For the classical Augustinian (and later Thomistic) approach to the Trinity was confirmed by a series of regional church councils in the West but never debated in a major church council with bishops and theologians from the East. Eventually, when Western missionaries began preaching the Gospel to Christians in Bulgaria quite close to Constantinople (modern day Istanbul), Photius, the patriarch of Constantinople, wrote an encyclical letter in 867 to the other bishops in the East warning them of the heresy of the Western missionaries.

---

[34] Ibid., 197.

This flare-up of tensions between East and West was eventually resolved by the Fourth Council of Constantinople (869–70), and peace between Rome and Constantinople was restored. But in 1009 the dispute arose all over again, and in 1054, with both sides excommunicating one another, the split was complete. In all honesty, this entire dispute was largely carried on by feuding church leaders and rival theologians; it had little immediate practical consequences for the faithful in both the East and West. But it did over time contribute to a significant difference in liturgy and church discipline for ordinary Christians on both sides, so that Eastern Christians would today feel a bit strange at a Roman Catholic Mass in the West, and Western Christians would feel correspondingly out of place attending a Eucharist in a contemporary Greek or Russian Orthodox Church.

Conclusion

So in the end doctrinal differences do make a difference. But the net result of the debate between bishops and theologians on both sides was to end up treating the doctrine of the Trinity mostly as an academic question and not as a pastoral reality of keen interest to all Christians. As we shall see in the next chapter, the focus of attention among Western philosophers and theologians in the late Middle Ages and in the early modern period shifted to God as one and infinite, beyond human comprehension. After all, if Christians can feel the presence of God in personal prayer and in reflection on the laws of nature, why worry about the inner divine life?

Chapter Three

Mysticism and Rationalism

In the late Middle Ages and the early modern period of Western Europe the classical doctrine of the Trinity that had been so carefully worked out by Aquinas and others was challenged, even called into question in some cases, on two fronts. The first such development was the new popularity of works in mystical theology where the focus was clearly more on spirituality, growing in the love of God, than on speculative theology, knowledge of the inner life of the triune God. The second was a new interest in empirical natural science in which God was viewed as the transcendent source of the laws of nature. God as Trinity thus became subordinate in the minds of many early natural scientists to God simply as a divine Agent at work in creation so as to guarantee its uniform operation. Both of these developments could be seen as offering new insights into the being and activity of God in this world. But, as we shall see below, when pursued in independence of the classical doctrine of the Trinity, the developments paved the way for the emergence first of pantheism (the virtual identification of God with the world) and then even of atheism (the belief that nature is all there is). The classical doctrine of the Trinity had perhaps overemphasized the transcendence of the triune God. The subtle temptation in some forms of late medieval mysticism and in early modern natural science, however, was to eliminate virtually all reference to the supernatural as a significant factor in human thought and behavior.

Accordingly, in this chapter we will first examine the writings of a few late medieval and early modern Christian mystics in order to see how their basic approach to God differed from that of the theologians mentioned in the preceding chapters. Then we will review the rapid development of early modern science in Western Europe, noting how with the eclipse of the doctrine of the Trinity in the minds of many prominent scientists, theism was replaced first by deism and then in some quarters by explicit atheism. As in the preceding chapters, however, we can only choose representative thinkers for our brief overview and make only tentative comments as a result.

The Cloud of Unknowing

Our starting point for the overview of the mystical tradition will be two English mystics of the late Middle Ages, the anonymous author of *The Cloud of Unknowing* and Julian of Norwich. As James Walsh makes clear in his introductory comments, the author of *The Cloud of Unknowing* was probably a Carthusian priest in fourteenth-century England who drew up a guide for the contemplative life to assist a young recruit for the same solitary life as himself.[1] Hence, both the spiritual director and the one being directed were Christians well versed in the beliefs and practices of Christianity. What the aspiring young man had to decide, however, was whether he was being called to the special form of con-templative prayer already practiced by the director. "Our minds are defeated when we try to draw close to God; only love can take the final step, drawing us into the dark yet dazzling mystery of God, as he is in himself."[2] Thus, one must feel called by divine grace to make this "leap of love." The cloud of unknowing, therefore, refers to the way in which the individual at prayer must put aside all thoughts and images of earthly things so as to focus on the reality of God alone.[3] One should not con-sciously entertain even thoughts and images of Jesus as the Incarnate Word, God the Father, or the Holy Spirit. One should patiently wait in mental darkness until "you experience in your will a simple reaching out to God."[4] Such a spiritual impulse toward God will not last more than a moment and will inevitably be followed by more mundane thoughts and desires. But if one is prepared to wait in the darkness for these "sparks" of divine love, within a single hour of prayer quite a number can be experienced so as spontaneously to detach the self from created things and lift it to union with God.[5]

[1] *The Cloud of Unknowing*, ed. James Walsh, SJ (New York: Paulist Press, 1981), 2–11.

[2] Simon Tugwell, OP, preface to *The Cloud of Unknowing*, xiv.

[3] *The Cloud of Unknowing*, chap. 3, p. 120.

[4] Ibid.

[5] Ibid., chap. 4, p. 126.

There is clearly an affinity here with earlier Christian spirituality as shaped by Neoplatonism, the ancient philosophy that emphasized the emanation of the world of creation from the utterly transcendent One and the gradual return to the One on the part of human beings through proper spiritual discipline.[6] But, as Simon Tugwell points out, the author of *The Cloud of Unknowing* was aware of the need for a balance in assessing the proper relation between the natural and the supernatural: "The ascent to the high point where God dwells in the dark cloud of mystery, though it does involve a certain transcending of creatures, does not annihilate them. Rather it guarantees that creation will be left intact in its own proper integrity."[7] The love of God within our hearts is not in competition with our human loves and desires but orders those loves and desires to itself and human beings to one another, giving us a strong sense of inner peace and harmony.[8]

Yet the author of the treatise also counsels: "[Y]ou must destroy all knowing and feeling of every kind of creature, but most especially of yourself."[9] This leads him to affirm a few chapters later that, in comparison with sensible objects that are specifically located in space and time, God is nowhere and nothing. Likewise, the contemplative should in this way learn to think of himself or herself as likewise nowhere and nothing.[10] Such an experience of nothingness, of course, can also be self-induced and not represent an experience of God at all, as the author himself concedes.[11] There is then both a likeness and a notable difference between this Christian experience of God and oneself as nowhere and nothing and the classical Buddhist experience of Absolute Nothingness and the "no-self."[12] Thus, while very precious and a sign of God's favor, mystical experiences such as those described by the author of *The Cloud of Unknowing* should be carefully monitored and analyzed, whenever possible, by a competent spiritual director.[13]

---

[6] See Tugwell, preface to *The Cloud of Unknowing*, xvi; likewise, Ivor Leclerc, *The Nature of Physical Existence* (New York: Humanities Press, 1972), 59–69.

[7] Tugwell, preface to *The Cloud of Unknowing*, xvii.

[8] *The Cloud of Unknowing*, chap. 24, pp. 169–70.

[9] Ibid., chap. 43, p. 202.

[10] Ibid., chap. 68, pp. 251–52.

[11] Ibid., chaps. 45–46, pp. 205–9.

[12] See, e.g., Joseph A. Bracken, SJ, *The Divine Matrix: Creativity as the Link Between East and West* (Eugene, OR: Wipf and Stock, 2006), 93–111.

[13] *The Cloud of Unknowing*, chap. 75, pp. 263–66.

The Trinitarian Spirituality of Julian of Norwich

In reflecting on the mystical experiences of Julian of Norwich, another English mystic of the fourteenth century, however, one notes an unmistakably trinitarian spirituality at work. Julian was a woman living in solitude as a layperson (not as a nun or woman religious). She seems to have been well acquainted with the great mystical writers of the Middle Ages and employed their wisdom in interpreting her own experiences. As Jean Leclerq, OSB, makes clear in his preface to the record of her mystical experiences, "Julian touches on all the main issues of theology, e.g., creation, man, nature, life, the Incarnation, the death and glorification of Christ, grace, sin, the Church, Mary and the world to come. Her primary focus, however, is on three great mysteries, or rather three aspects of the same mystery: God, man and their reconciliation."[14] Yet there were also tensions present in her prayer and reflection, as she evidently struggled to reconcile traditional church teaching with her own mystical experiences.

For example, Julian was greatly preoccupied with the apparent contradiction between her experiences of God's loving care for us sinners and the demands of God's justice. Incorrigible sinners will end up in hell. Likewise, while she had supreme confidence that "all will be well,"[15] Julian herself had a dream in which the devil tormented her.[16] But afterward Jesus appeared to her and assured her that, while she may be tormented by the devil on occasion, she will not be overcome: "God wants us to pay attention to his words, and always to be strong in our certainty, in well-being and in woe, for he loves us and delights in us, and so he wishes us to love him and delight in him and trust greatly in him, and all will be well."[17] In still another text, she makes reference to the "great deed" that the blessed Trinity will perform on the last day: "For just as the blessed Trinity created all things from nothing, just so will the same blessed Trinity make everything well which is not well."[18] But then she

---

[14] Jean Leclerq, OSB, preface to Julian of Norwich, *Showings*, trans. Edmund Colledge, OSA, and James Walsh, SJ (New York: Paulist, 1978), 6.

[15] Julian, *Showings* (Short Text), chap. 16, p. 153. NB: There are two versions of the *Showings*, the second much longer than the first and, as Edmund Colledge indicates in the introduction, representing Julian's more mature thinking on the problem of good and evil (ibid., 23–24).

[16] Ibid., chap. 21, p. 163; see also *Showings* (Long Text), chap. 67, pp. 311–12.

[17] *Showings* (Short Text), chap. 22, p. 165.

[18] *Showings* (Long Text), chap. 32, p. 233.

recalls the teaching of the church that many creatures will be damned (fallen angels, pagans, unfaithful Christians). Yet from the Lord she receives the response: "What is impossible to you is not impossible to me. I shall preserve my word in everything, and I shall make everything well."[19]

Edmund Colledge points out that in the longer version of *Showings* Julian has an elaborate parable on the mercy of God the Father toward Adam, both as an individual and as representative of fallen humanity.[20] Jesus identifies with Adam and accepts the blame for our sinful human condition: "And so has our good Lord Jesus taken upon him[self] all our blame; and therefore our Father may not, does not wish to assign more blame to us than to his own beloved Son Jesus Christ."[21] In this context, Julian introduces the metaphor for which she is perhaps most famous. She first suggests that God is both our Father and our Mother.[22] But then she specifies that Christ as our Savior and Redeemer is our Mother: "Jesus Christ, who opposes good to evil, is our true Mother. We have our being from him, where the foundation of motherhood begins, with all the sweet protection of love which endlessly follows."[23] As Jean Leclerq comments, what Julian develops here "is not the idea of femininity as opposed to or distinct from that of masculinity, but that of the motherhood of God as complement to that of his fatherhood. . . . In no way does she wish to substitute the idea of the motherhood of God for that of his fatherhood; she wants to unite them."[24] As we shall see in chapter 7, Elizabeth Johnson and other contemporary Christian feminists are trying to accomplish something similar with their rethinking of the traditional "names" of the divine persons so as to allow for both masculine and feminine images of God.

The German Mystical Tradition: Meister Eckhart

Mystically oriented spirituality also flowered outside of England in the late Middle Ages. One of the key figures in Germany was unquestionably Meister Eckhart, who like Thomas Aquinas was a Dominican priest but was a full generation younger than Aquinas. In addition, as I have made

[19] Ibid.
[20] Colledge, introduction, p. 24; *Showings* (Long Text), chap. 51, pp. 267–78.
[21] Ibid., p. 275.
[22] Ibid., chap. 52, p. 279.
[23] Ibid., chap. 59, p. 295.
[24] Ibid., preface, p. 11.

clear elsewhere,[25] while Eckhart used the terminology of Aquinas and other scholastic thinkers of his day, his basic mind-set was different than theirs. Much of his theology was worked out in terms of sermons to women religious who were seeking direction in their spiritual life. As a result, his focus was on subjective experience rather than on objective cause-effect relations as in the theology of Aquinas. One of Eckhart's key concepts, for example, was the notion of *ground*: the ground of the divine being and the ground of the soul within human beings. But by "ground" he did not mean in the first place "reason" or external cause, but rather "vital source" or inner cause, that which inwardly empowers someone or something to exist and to act in a certain way. Thus he got into trouble with ecclesiastical authorities by claiming that the ground of the divine being and the ground of the soul within human beings are one and the same. Yet, as Bernard McGinn comments,[26] Eckhart was not a pantheist, one who believes that God and the world are different names for the same reality. No, according to Eckhart, God and human beings are totally different and yet they share a common ground of being or source of vital activity, as he makes clear in Sermon 6:

> The Father gives birth to his Son in eternity, equal to himself. "The Word was with God, and God was the Word" (John 1:1); it was the same in the same nature. Yet I say more: He has given birth to him in my soul. Not only is the soul with him and he equal with it, but he is in it, and the Father gives his Son birth in the soul in the same way as he gives him birth in eternity, and not otherwise. He must do it whether he likes it or not . . . I say more: He gives me birth, me, his Son and the same Son. I say more: He gives birth not only to me, His Son, but he gives birth to me as himself and himself as me and to me as his being and nature. In the innermost source, there I spring out in the Holy Spirit, where there is one life and one being and one work.[27]

As McGinn and others have commented, there was a long-standing tradition in ancient and medieval Christian theology that through divine grace God the Son can be born in the human soul.[28] But Eckhart in this

---

[25] Bracken, *The Divine Matrix*, 38–45.

[26] Bernard McGinn, introduction to *Meister Eckhart: The Essential Sermons, Commentaries, Treatises, and Defense* (New York: Paulist, 1981), 61.

[27] *Meister Eckhart*, 187.

[28] McGinn, introduction, 50.

citation goes far beyond conventional Christian theology. For he identifies himself not only with the Son but with the Father and the Holy Spirit as well, in effect, with the entire Trinity dwelling by grace within his soul.

What must be remembered, of course, is that Eckhart is referring to a unity of activity, not a unity of being. The three divine persons and their rational creatures have the same ground of being even as they remain distinct from one another as Creator and creature. Within the Trinity itself, for example, there is a *bullitio* (literally, boiling) whereby the three divine persons emerge as distinct persons from their innermost source. But creation takes place when the *bullitio* becomes an *ebullitio* (literally, boiling over).[29] One and the same activity is thus the vital source of the life of the three divine persons within the Trinity and the dynamic ground for the existence of creation, above all, the life of the soul in union with the persons of the Trinity. For the same reason, in Sermon 52 Eckhart claims that in that innermost source of God's own being he [Eckhart] has always existed and was the cause of his own existence in this world: "I am the cause of myself in the order of my being, which is eternal, and not in the order of becoming, which is temporal. And therefore I am unborn, and in the manner in which I am unborn I can never die. In my unborn manner I have been eternally, and am now, and shall eternally remain. What I am in the order of having been born, that will die and perish, for it is mortal, and so it must in time suffer corruption."[30]

Understandably, these statements by Eckhart alarmed church authorities in Cologne where he was living and preaching. The statements clearly smacked of pantheism, the elimination of any distinction between God and ourselves, God and the world. But the authorities were even more disturbed by Eckhart's further claim that one should pray to God to be free of "God," understood as the Creator of heaven and earth, so as to "break through" into unity with the innermost source of the divine being where God is what God is apart from creation.[31] Only then is one fully detached from one's self and fully absorbed into the all-encompassing reality of the divine being. But this would seem to imply that one can more or less dispense with the normal sacramental life of the church in which the focus is on the activity of the divine persons in the creation and redemption of the world. One's striving is for an immediate experience of God in the divine ground of being where the distinction of the

[29] Ibid., 37.
[30] *Meister Eckhart*, 202–3.
[31] Ibid., 200.

divine persons from one another is no longer a factor. One is genuinely detached, truly "poor," when one is absorbed into the Godhead, the divine ground of being, without remainder: "And when this detachment ascends to the highest place, it knows nothing of knowing, it loves nothing of loving, and from light it becomes dark. To this we can also apply what one teacher says: 'The poor in spirit are those who have abandoned all things for God, just as they were his when we did not even exist.'"[32]

Teresa of Avila: An Early Modern Spanish Mystic

As we have seen already in analyzing *The Cloud of Unknowing*, there can be difficulty here in deciding whether such an experience of nothingness is truly an experience of God or simply of nothingness apart from God, and whether it is a self-induced natural experience or one to which the individual is led by divine grace, the invisible activity of the Holy Spirit in one's soul. In this sense, it is reassuring to examine the writings of another female mystic in the Christian tradition, St. Teresa of Avila (1515–82) , for whom the experience of God as Trinity represented the highest reaches of contemplative prayer. Unlike Julian of Norwich, Teresa was a member of a community of women religious (Carmelites) rather than a laywoman living in solitude. And unlike Julian she spent a great deal of time outside her cell in the convent, traveling about Spain in the process of the reform of the Carmelite order, which she undertook with the help of St. John of the Cross. But like Julian she had a very serious physical illness as a young woman, which gave rise to a much more intense life of prayer on her part afterward.

Teresa wrote several books on the basis of her own spiritual experiences. The most famous is certainly *The Interior Castle*, written in 1577 toward the end of her life.[33] In it Teresa describes growth in the contemplative life as a progressive movement inward through seven "dwelling places" toward full union with the triune God at the very center of one's soul. Passage through the first three dwelling places is achieved largely through personal effort. In the fourth dwelling place, however, the "prayer of quiet" is initiated, where the individual allows herself to be guided more and more by divine inspiration. But only in the fifth dwelling place are the mental faculties of mind and will sufficiently stilled so

[32] Ibid., 292–93. Reference is to Eckhart's essay *On Detachment*.

[33] Teresa of Avila, *The Interior Castle*, trans. Kieran Kavanaugh, OCD, and Otilio Rodriguez, OCD (New York: Paulist, 1979).

that when the soul returns to normal consciousness "it can in no way doubt that it was in God and God was in it."[34] In the sixth dwelling place, says Teresa, the soul is now "wounded with love for its Spouse."[35] That is, it experiences "raptures" when the spirit feels itself outside the body in union with the risen Lord but also experiences the pain of withdrawal when the rapture is ended. Finally, in the seventh dwelling place, the soul is at peace with a persistent awareness of its union with the three divine persons even in the midst of external occupations. Through what she calls an intellectual vision Teresa sees that "all three persons are one substance and one power and one knowledge and one God alone."[36]

As with Julian of Norwich, therefore, the mystical experience of Teresa was primarily interpersonal, with the focus on Jesus as the personal mediator between the triune God and herself. As Kieran Kavanaugh comments in the introduction to *The Interior Castle*, Teresa was most insistent that "an effort to forget Christ and live in continual absorption in the divinity will result in a failure to enter the last two dwelling places."[37] Furthermore, like her countryman Ignatius of Loyola, who himself was favored with mystical experiences of the Trinity, Teresa was always on her guard against the deception of the devil in spiritual matters, learning to practice what Ignatius called "the discernment of spirits."[38] In some ways even more troublesome, she found herself getting bad spiritual advice from priest confessors. In her view, a learned man was better than a spiritual person, but one who was both learned and spiritual was best of all.[39] As Evelyn Underhill comments, Teresa counted Jesuits, members of the religious community of men founded by Ignatius, as some of her most trusted advisers.[40]

Thus far in this chapter we have reviewed the contribution of four celebrated late medieval and early modern mystics to the Christian understanding of God. On the one hand, in the writings of Julian of Norwich and Teresa of Avila we have seen how mystical experience can add warmth and personal feeling to the otherwise abstract and impersonal

---

[34] Ibid., Bk. 5, chap. 1:8, p. 89.

[35] Ibid., Bk. 6, chap. 1:1, p. 108.

[36] Ibid., Bk. 7, chap. 1:6, p. 175.

[37] Ibid., p. 27.

[38] Cf., e.g., *The Spiritual Exercises of Saint Ignatius*, trans. George E. Ganss, SJ (Chicago: Loyola University Press, 1992), 121–28, 189–95.

[39] Teresa of Avila, *The Interior Castle*, Bk. 6, chap. 8:8, p. 154.

[40] Evelyn Underhill, *The Mystics of the Church* (New York: Schocken Books, 1964), 171–72.

logic of the classical doctrine of the Trinity. On the other hand, in *The Cloud of Unknowing* and the writings of Meister Eckhart, we see how ambiguity can arise about the type of experience one is really having: a genuine experience of God or a trance-like experience of nothingness in the purely natural order.

The New Approach to Science

In the remaining pages of this chapter I turn to the second major influence on the classical doctrine of God in the late medieval and early modern period of Western history: the rise of natural science and the new recourse to mathematics for the explanation of the workings of nature. Here especially the classical trinitarian doctrine of God was left in the background as educated people focused more and more on the new image of God as the Architect of the universe or, in mathematical terms, the Great Geometer.

Nicholas of Cusa: Mystic and Mathematician

Curiously, however, the groundwork for this new approach to the God-world relationship was laid by a late medieval mystic, Nicholas of Cusa (1401–64). Truly a "Renaissance Man," Nicholas was a noted canon lawyer, bishop, and cardinal, active in preparing for the Council of Florence and the possible reconciliation of the Eastern and Western Christian churches (cf. chap. 2). At the same time, he wrote a number of works in philosophy, theology, and mathematics, most notably *De docta Ignorantia* (*On Learned Ignorance*) in which he argued that human beings have no conceptual knowledge of God but must use humanly contrived symbols to point to the absolute infinity of God.[41] Unlike Aquinas, who deduced the infinity of God from the need for a causal explanation of our human experience of finitude, Nicholas of Cusa argued for a mystical intuition into the absolute unity of God as the "Coincidence of Opposites."[42] If God is thus the perfect integration of all diversities and oppositions to be found in this world, then the world must exist in God in much the

---

[41] See the introduction to *Nicholas of Cusa on Learned Ignorance*, trans. Jasper Hopkins (Minneapolis, MN: Arthur Banning Press, 1981), 4.

[42] Ibid., Bk. 1, chap. 4 (53–54). As Hopkins notes in the introduction, the phrase "coincidence of opposites" does not appear as such in *On Learned Ignorance* but is implied in his analysis of the "Maximum" (6).

same way that the shapes of a triangle, circle, and sphere are implicitly "enfolded" within the image of an infinitely extended straight line. Yet these same geometrical figures can be subsequently "unfolded" so as to take their proper form as distinct from the figure of a straight line.[43] God, therefore, is the source of all things and in all things.[44] God and the world, however, are different in that God is an Absolute Infinity and the world is a "contracted" Infinity.[45] The world, in other words, is infinitely extended in space and time. Yet God as Absolute Infinity is not in any sense extended but, rather, totally transcendent of space and time.

Perhaps without fully realizing it, Nicholas of Cusa thereby overturned the medieval worldview, which was governed by precise cause-effect relations between God as Creator and the world of creation. Whereas Aquinas had argued for the transcendence of God to the world and yet for the immanence of God in the world as its First Efficient Cause, Transcendent Formal Cause, and Ultimate Final Cause,[46] Cusa argued for an infinite difference between God and the world so that we human beings can know nothing directly about God except that God as Absolute Infinity contains the relative infinity of the world in all its diversity. We have, accordingly, only a symbolic understanding of God, a "learned ignorance" of the divine being. With respect to our knowledge of the world, however, the situation is entirely different: if the world is a "contracted" infinity and if this infinity is expressed in terms of space and time, then we know that the key feature of physical reality is that it is extended and by implication capable of precise analysis in mathematical terms.

Descartes and Newton

This new emphasis on mathematics as the key to understanding physical reality is confirmed in the writings of Rene Descartes and Isaac Newton, albeit in somewhat different ways. Descartes was primarily a mathematician with a passion for certitude.[47] Hence, he began his philo-

---

[43] Ibid., chaps. 13, 14, 15 (63–66).

[44] Ibid., Bk. 2, chap. 3 (95–96).

[45] Ibid., chap. 4 (96–98).

[46] See Aquinas, *Summa Theologiae*, I, question 2, art. 3: the "Five Ways" to "prove" the existence of God.

[47] See Michael J. Buckley, SJ, *At the Origins of Modern Atheism* (New Haven, CN: Yale University Press, 1987), 69–73.

sophical system with an unquestionable truth, "I think; therefore, I am."[48]
But the existence of an external world apart from the self is still something one can doubt. Thus to guarantee the objective reality of the external world, Descartes appealed to the existence of God as someone who
cannot deceive us in the use of our God-given mental powers. Descartes
was already certain that God exists, since in his mind the idea of the
Infinite is logically prior to the idea of the finite. Everything in human
experience is finite or limited. Therefore, if we have a clear and distinct
idea of the Infinite, it must come from God who once again cannot
deceive us.[49] Still another "clear and distinct" idea for Descartes was that
matter is synonymous with extension, that is, with what can be measured
mathematically.[50] But if matter is simply what can be measured, then we
live in a mechanical universe that "can be explained simply by matter
and the [mathematical] laws of nature."[51] The world then tells us virtually nothing about the reality of God as its Creator.

The similarity to the thought of Nicholas of Cusa is clear. God as
infinite is absolutely transcendent of the world; the world as finite symbolically reflects the infinity of God but is humanly understandable only
in mathematical terms, which, of course, have no direct application to
the spiritual being and activity of God. With the adoption of mathematics
as a tool for the analysis of physical reality, then, the world is effectively
"godless." Isaac Newton, to be sure, made room for God in his understanding of physical reality. As a physicist interested in determining the
laws governing the motion of physical bodies (above all, the motion of
the earth and the other planets around the sun), Newton claimed that
God is needed first to set in motion and then to govern the movements
of these same physical bodies: "God in the sense of the dominion or force
from which the world issues is obvious for Newton and inescapable as
the rational consequence of a system of the world."[52] But Newton's
concept of God is strictly unipersonal; it is not the trinitarian God of
orthodox Christian theology. In fact, in his extensive theological writings
Newton was a fierce opponent of the classical doctrine of the Trinity and

[48] Rene Descartes, *Meditations concerning First Philosophy*, II, in *Rene Descartes: Discourse
on Method and Meditations*, trans. Laurence J. Lafleur (Indianapolis, IN: Bobbs-Merrill,
1960), 82.

[49] Ibid., III, Lafleur, 101.

[50] Ibid., VI, Lafleur, 126–43.

[51] Buckley, *At the Origins of Modern Atheism*, 97.

[52] Ibid., 138–39.

belief in the divinity of Jesus.[53] Therefore, by conceiving the world as a cosmic machine run by unvarying mathematical laws, and thinking of God as a unipersonal cosmic designer or "clockmaker," Newton paved the way first for deism and ultimately for atheism as the rational way to explain how nature works.

From Theism, to Deism, to Atheism

Perhaps the easiest way to distinguish between the terms "theism," "deism," and "atheism" is to take note of Denis Diderot, the celebrated French philosopher of the eighteenth century. In his early years Diderot was a student of the Jesuits at Langres, France, and even considered entering the Society of Jesus as a novice. At that time he was presumably a theist, one who believed in a personal God active in this world. After studies at the University of Paris, he became for a short time a deist, one who believed in a Creator God who never interfered in the operation of the laws that he had set up for the world.[54] But Diderot became a convinced atheist when it dawned on him that matter is active, not passive; matter is thus capable of self-generation. "Matter is no longer the inert, geometric extension of Descartes, nor the Newtonian mass identified with inertia and known only through its resistance to change. Now matter is the creative source of all change,"[55] and a Creator God is no longer needed as an explanation for the way things are in this world.

Naturally, there was intense opposition both from the institutional church and from individual believers to the outspoken atheism of Diderot, Baron d'Holbach, and other *philosophes* within the French Enlightenment. But the long-term effect upon practicing scientists was to encourage them to think that physics and theology are academic disciplines that should be kept separate from one another since neither one can contribute significantly to the advance of knowledge in the other. The famous French scientist Pierre Laplace, for example, corrected the periodic irregularities in the celestial mechanics of Newton without reference to God and devised a "nebular" hypothesis for the origin of the solar system.[56] As Michael

---

[53] See Richard S. Westfall, "Isaac Newton," in *Science and Religion: A Historical Introduction*, ed. Gary B. Ferngren (Baltimore, MD: Johns Hopkins University Press, 2002), 156.

[54] Buckley, *At the Origins of Modern Atheism*, 197–211.

[55] Ibid., 249.

[56] Ronald L. Numbers, "Cosmogonies," in *Science and Religion*, 239.

Buckley comments, Laplace was thereby no more "atheistic" in his thinking than Descartes, who likewise insisted that rational, purely objective principles of mechanics govern what happens in this world.[57] But Laplace differed from both Descartes and Newton in insisting that theology has no role to play within physics and the other natural sciences. In many ways, that assumption is still operative in the minds of many scientists (and at least some theologians) to this day.

Conclusion

In part 3 of this book I will make clear how a revised approach to the doctrine of the Trinity could well be the key to a better understanding of the God-world relationship in the light of contemporary evolutionary theory. But as this brief historical overview, first of late medieval mysticism and then of early modern scientific rationalism, should have made clear, by the end of the Enlightenment in Western Europe the classical doctrine of the Trinity no longer occupied center stage in the minds of most Christian philosophers and theologians. In the face of widespread skepticism about the role of religion in public life and even about the possibility of a rational "proof" for the existence of God, only two alternatives remained for most educated Christians. The first alternative, represented by the philosopher Immanuel Kant in his *Critique of Practical Reason*, was basically to reduce religion to morality and argue that God exists to guarantee eternal happiness for the morally righteous.[58] That is, since there is no assurance in this life that good will ultimately triumph over evil, there must be a God to uphold public morality, or social chaos will inevitably result. The other alternative, represented by Friedrich Schleiermacher and other Protestant theologians, was to ground proof for the existence of God and the supernatural order in subjective feeling rather than objective reason. That is, since feeling is always present in our human awareness of self, other human beings, and the world at large, God is present in human consciousness on a feeling level as the Absolute Other. Proof for the existence of God, therefore, is to be found not in logical inference but in the feeling of absolute dependence on God

---

[57] Buckley, *At the Origins of Modern Atheism*, 325.

[58] Ibid., 327–30. Reference is to Immanuel Kant, *Critique of Practical Philosophy and Other Writings in Moral Philosophy*, trans. Lewis White Beck (Chicago: University of Chicago Press, 1949), 227–28.

as the transcendent Other in one's life.[59] In the next chapter we will see how Karl Barth challenged both Kant and Schleiermacher on these philosophical assumptions about the God-world relationship. In his view all three divine persons are at work in the act of revelation, the ongoing communication of God's Word to creatures.

---

[59] Buckley, *At the Origins of Modern Atheism*, 330–32. Reference is to Friedrich Schleiermacher, *The Christian Faith*, eds. H.R. Mackintosh & J.S. Stewart (Edinburgh: T&T Clark, 1976), 12–18.

Chapter Four

Recovery of the Doctrine of the Trinity in the Twentieth Century

Not often does a country pastor with a single published work on the New Testament shake up the world of academic theology of his day so completely as did Karl Barth (1886–1968) with his commentary on St. Paul's Epistle to the Romans in 1918. In Barth's own words, he wrote it "with a joyful sense of discovery," finding new meaning for himself and his readers in the ancient text.[1] But with his strong emphasis on the priority of divine revelation to human reason in the interpretation of Scripture, he challenged the presuppositions of liberal Protestant theology since the time of Schleiermacher a hundred years earlier. As Barth notes in the preface to the second revised edition of the commentary, his effort therein is to make clear the "infinite qualitative" distinction between time and eternity that can only be bridged by an act of divine revelation in the person of Jesus Christ.[2]

In this way he expressed his uneasiness both with the style of biblical criticism in his day and with efforts by Schleiermacher and others to ground systematic theology primarily in human experience rather than in the literal text of the Bible. When others complained that Barth was thereby reading his own meaning into the words of Scripture, his counterargument was that in their preoccupation with peripheral textual issues

---

[1] Karl Barth, preface to the first edition of *The Epistle to the Romans*, 6th ed., trans. Edwyn C. Hoskyns (London: Oxford University Press, 1933), 2.

[2] Ibid., 10.

and background information, many Scripture scholars were ignoring the core of Paul's message about God's self-revelation in Christ, which should be as valid today as it was for Paul's contemporaries in the first century of the Christian era. But it was the starting point of human experience for the interpretation of Scripture that Barth found especially repugnant, for it effectively ignored the "infinite qualitative distinction between time and eternity," creation and its creator, spoken of above. In this respect, he was equally critical of traditional Roman Catholic theology that from the time of Thomas Aquinas grounded theology in philosophy, specifically, in the analogy of being, the movement of thought from the human experience of the finite to a qualified understanding of the infinite. Rather, for Barth, God is infinitely beyond being insofar as human beings can comprehend it. Nothing in this world can, therefore, provide true insight into the transcendent reality of God. Genuine Christian theology must be grounded in God's Word: in the first place, the person of Christ, and then, the text of Sacred Scripture.

Karl Barth's Approach to the Doctrine of the Trinity

Given his celebrity status as the author of a controversial Scripture commentary, Barth was offered an honorary chair in Reformed Theology at the University of Gottingen in 1921. Later he accepted professorial positions first at Münster and then at Bonn. It was during his tenure at Bonn that he began the major work of his life, the *Church Dogmatics*, a systematic approach to what he called Evangelical Theology, in the face of both modern secularism and, above all for his German readers, the rise of National Socialism (Adolph Hitler and the Nazi Party). In these pages we will consider only his explanation of the doctrine of the Trinity, which stands at the beginning of the *Church Dogmatics*.

Barth begins by noting that not all talk about God in the church is proclamation of the Word of God.[3] Theology and catechetics, for example, are not proclamation of the Word in the strict sense since they are more human speech and reflection about God than proclamation of the Word that originates with God:

> Proclamation is human speech in and by which God Himself speaks like a king through the mouth of his herald, and which is meant to

[3] Karl Barth, *Church Dogmatics*, vol. 1, part 1, eds. G. W. Bromiley and T. F. Torrance, trans. G. W. Bromiley (Edinburgh: T&T Clark, 1975), 49–51.

be heard and accepted as speech in and by which God Himself speaks, and therefore heard and accepted in faith as divine decision concerning life and death, as divine judgment and pardon, eternal Law and eternal Gospel both together.[4]

Proclamation of the Word, accordingly, is done only in a spirit of faith and obedience, principally through preaching, but also through sacrament, the eucharistic liturgy.[5] There are, to be sure, three expressions of the Word of God: the revealed Word of God in the person of Jesus, the written Word of God in Sacred Scripture, and the preached Word of God here and now in the context of the sacred liturgy. But all three are one in the event of proclamation.[6] Furthermore, one recognizes it as the Word of God through listening to it in faith under the inspiration of the Holy Spirit: "It is on our lips and in our hearts as the mystery of the Spirit who is the Lord."[7] Neither historical criticism (as in Liberal Protestantism) nor the teaching authority of the church (as in Roman Catholicism) can thus take precedence over God's self-attestation in the event of proclamation.

Within this context we can now understand Barth's explanation of the doctrine of the Trinity as the necessary presupposition of the event of proclamation: "If we really want to understand revelation in terms of its subject, i.e., God, then the first thing that we have to realize is that this subject, God, the Revealer, is identical with His act in revelation and also identical with its effect."[8] Thus the "root" of the doctrine of the Trinity is to be found in the act of revelation. God is the Revealer (God the Father), the One Revealed (God the Son) and the act of revealing (God the Holy Spirit), all at the same time. God is thus one God in three ways or modes of being: "in the mode of the Father, in the mode of the Son, and in the mode of the Holy Ghost."[9] Barth prefers the expression "mode of being" to "person" because it does not thereby lend itself to tritheism, the notion of three gods in close collaboration, but instead insists that God is "one divine I" in threefold repetition.[10] Yet these three "modes of being" fully share in one another's being and activity, both within the inner life of God and in the work of creation, redemption, and

---

[4] Ibid., 52.
[5] Ibid., 56.
[6] Ibid., 120–21.
[7] Ibid., 186.
[8] Ibid., 296.
[9] Ibid., 359.
[10] Ibid., 351.

sanctification toward us their creatures. Barth here endorses the notion of *perichoresis* as set forth by St. John Damascene.[11]

Eberhard Jüngel and Karl Rahner

Barth's emphasis on the doctrine of the Trinity as rooted in the very concept of divine revelation had an enormous impact on subsequent Protestant theology. Eberhard Jüngel, for example, in his books *The Doctrine of the Trinity* and *God as the Mystery of the World*, further explored the notion of a correspondence between the immanent Trinity (the inner life of the three divine persons apart from creation) and the economic Trinity (the three divine persons as active in the creation, redemption, and sanctification of the world).[12] With Barth he claims that God is intrinsically "self-related." That is, unlike human beings who only over time acquire relations with others, God cannot exist except as a relational reality, three dynamically interrelated "modes of being" or ways of being God, both within the inner life of the Trinity and in dealing with the world of creation.[13] But, granted that there is a deep connection between the inner life of the three divine persons and their dealing with us their creatures, does this mean that God needs us in order to be God as much as we need God in order to be ourselves? The Lutheran theologian Ted Peters seems to say yes: "[h]owever we define God, we must include the experience of the human Jesus in the definition. And because the human Jesus represents the incarnation—that is, God in the world—one would expect that God's relationship to the world would become constitutive of God's being, or better, becoming."[14] But, as we will see below, not everyone would agree.

Karl Rahner, for example, perhaps the best known Catholic theologian of the twentieth century, in his book *The Trinity* initially complained that Christians in their devotional life are mere "monotheists" because their prayer is directed simply to "God" rather than to Father, Son, and Holy Spirit.[15] It is as if any one of the divine persons could have become human

---

[11] Ibid., 370–71. See also above, chap. 2.

[12] Eberhard Jüngel, *The Doctrine of God: God's Being is in Becoming* (Grand Rapids, MI; Eerdmans, 1976), esp. 68–83; *God as the Mystery of the World* (Grand Rapids, MI: Eerdmans, 1983), 368–96. See also Ted Peters, *God as Trinity: Relationality and Temporality in Divine Life* (Louisville, KY: Westminster/John Knox, 1993), 90–96, for a convenient summary of Jüngel's position.

[13] Jüngel, *The Doctrine of the Trinity*, 63–64; 89–108.

[14] Peters, *God as Trinity*, 91.

[15] Rahner, *The Trinity*, 10–11.

in order to redeem us. As a result, the classical Western understanding of the Trinity as formulated by Thomas Aquinas is too abstract and speculative to inspire devotion to each of the divine persons individually. One hopes one day to go to heaven and enjoy the Beatific Vision. But will it be a Vision of three divine persons in their relations to one another and to us their creatures or simply a Vision of God in some generic sense that allows us to feel "saved"?

Rahner's own position, akin to that of Barth, is that only the Son of God could have become human because only the Son is the Divine Word, the eternal self-expression of the Father that has become incarnate, taken flesh, in the person of Jesus. Thus, argues Rahner, the inner life of the three divine persons is revealed in both the teachings and the life of Jesus; in this sense, the "economic" Trinity (the Trinity at work in the world or the "economy" of salvation) is the "immanent" Trinity (the Trinity apart from the world) and vice versa.[16] But Rahner then adds: "God relates to us in a threefold manner, and this threefold, free, and gratuitous relation to us is not merely a copy or an analogy of the inner Trinity, but this Trinity itself, albeit as freely and gratuitously communicated."[17] The key words here are, of course, "freely and gratuitously communicated." This presupposes that the three divine persons have an interrelated existence proper to themselves apart from their relation to us their creatures. But once they freely choose to create and redeem us, they are present to us really as themselves and not in virtue of some finite copy or analogy of their inner divine life. The world of creation, accordingly, is really taken up into the life of God but in such a way as to respect the difference between time and eternity, life in this world and life after death in full union with the triune God.

Another way in which Rahner stays close to the classical understanding of the Trinity is in his insistence that, despite being involved in the history of this world through becoming incarnate in Jesus of Nazareth, the Divine Word did not change in his own being or in his eternal relation to the Father and the Spirit. "The mystery of the incarnation must lie in God himself: in the fact that he, though unchangeable 'in himself,' can become something [change] in another."[18] Only in his human nature, and thus not in his divine nature, is the Person of the Divine Word

---

[16] Ibid., 22.

[17] Ibid., 35.

[18] Peters, *God as Trinity*, 101. Reference is to Karl Rahner, "On the Theology of the Incarnation," in *Theological Investigations* IV, trans. Kevin Smyth (Baltimore: Helicon, 1966), 113–14, n. 3.

affected by entrance into human history with all its inevitable ups and downs, joys and sufferings. Peters may well be right in claiming a certain inconsistency on Rahner's part here. One cannot logically claim that the three divine persons, above all the Divine Word, are really involved in our world and yet are not personally affected by what happens here and now. But Peters may be overstating his case when he in turn claims that "the eternal or immanent Trinity finds its very identity in the economy of temporal salvation events."[19] "Very identity" seems to imply full identity so that the history of the world is the history of God and vice versa. God and the world are then part of one and the same cosmic process.

Catherine Mowry LaCugna: God for Us

As we will see in a subsequent chapter of this book, this is the understanding of the God-world relationship set forth by many contemporary philosophers and theologians, above all, process theologians who are followers of the English-American philosopher Alfred North Whitehead. But for the moment we will follow the line of argument presented by a Catholic theologian more in the classical tradition of trinitarian theology, namely, Catherine Mowry LaCugna. In her first major publication, *God for Us*, she created quite a stir in Catholic theological circles. For she argued that, beginning with the Council of Nicaea, the development of the doctrine of the Trinity has been a major mistake in that it effectively denied what the church fathers before Nicaea had in mind in defining the Trinity: that "God has given Godself to us in Jesus Christ and the Spirit, and this self-revelation or self-communication is nothing less than what God is as God. Creation, redemption, and consummation are thus anchored in God."[20] To recover the pristine understanding of the doctrine for Christian life, argues LaCugna, we must affirm the identity of the immanent Trinity and the economic Trinity much more strongly than Rahner, in effect, endorse the position of Ted Peters:

> There is neither an economic nor an immanent Trinity; there is only the *oikonomia* that is the concrete realization of the mystery of *theologia* in time, space, history, and personality. In this framework, the doctrine of the Trinity encompasses much more than the immanent

[19] Peters, *God as Trinity*, 97.

[20] Catherine Mowry LaCugna, *God for Us: The Trinity and Christian Life* (HarperCollins: San Francisco, 1991), 209.

Trinity, envisioned in static ahistorical and transeconomic terms; the subject matter of the Christian theology of God is the one dynamic movement of God, *a Patre ad Patrem* [from the Father to the Father].[21]

Many conservative Catholic theologians bristled at the idea that the development of the doctrine of the Trinity from the Council of Nicaea onward was simply a huge mistake. But the key issue is whether LaCugna was right in her judgment.

On the one hand, the immense popularity of her book indicates that she was "on target" in claiming that the classical explanation of the doctrine of the Trinity had little or no pastoral value because of its highly technical language. But, on the other hand, did she herself unconsciously overstate her case in claiming that the divine persons exist "for us"? Can anyone totally exist for another without having something of oneself to give to the other? Even if we presuppose that the divine persons are uniquely self-giving to one another and to their creatures, they cannot give away being Father, Son, and Holy Spirit, either to one another or to their creatures. So logically there has to be a Trinity apart from the world in order for the Trinity to be really present in the world.

One could counterargue, of course, that this is to misunderstand LaCugna's position. She only claims that "the mystery of *theologia* [the Christian doctrine of God] in time, space, history, and personality . . . is the one dynamic movement of God, *a Patre ad Patrem*." But without further qualification this smacks of pantheism. Either the divine life is absorbed into the cosmic process without remainder or the cosmic process is totally absorbed into the divine life. Somewhat akin to Neoplatonism as studied in chapter 2, the world then emanates from God and eventually returns to God, but without any real free choice either on the part of the divine persons or of ourselves as involved in the process.

Bernard Lonergan

Clearly this is not what LaCugna had in mind in publishing her book. But it does make clear how difficult it is to strike the right balance in thinking through the God-world relationship. Two more theologians, accordingly, may be cited before bringing this chapter to a close, since both in my judgment made an important contribution to trinitarian theology. The first was Bernard Lonergan, SJ, longtime professor of theology at the Gregorian University in Rome. His lecture notes on the doctrine

---

[21] Ibid., 223.

of the Trinity from a historical perspective were eventually published under the title *The Way to Nicea*.[22] Therein he celebrated what LaCugna came to regard as a major mistake, namely, the formulation of an understanding of the doctrine of the Trinity that stands on its own, possesses a logical consistency quite apart from any historical context or cultural bias. From the final paragraph of the book:

> For it [the Nicene dogma] marks a transition from multiplicity to unity: from a multiplicity of symbols, titles and predicates to the ultimate ground of all of these, namely, the Son's consubstantiality with the Father. Equally, it marks a transition from things as related to us to things as they are in themselves, from the relational concepts of God as supreme agent, Creator, Omnipotent Lord of all, to an ontological conception of the divine substance itself.[23]

Where LaCugna seeks to recover a relational understanding of God as known to us here and now, Lonergan sees in the Nicene definition of the consubstantiality of the Son with the Father an ontological assertion that transcends particular times and places because it is based on the actual reality of the triune God, quite apart from our human efforts to understand it. Lonergan thus seeks a scientific understanding of the Trinity, while LaCugna is interested in a contemporary pastoral understanding of the Trinity.

But who is right? Perhaps they are both right and both wrong, albeit for different reasons. LaCugna is certainly right in thinking that the classical formulation of the doctrine of the Trinity has become a virtual museum piece simply because it is so abstract and so far removed from the devotional life of Christians. How many Catholic priests and Protestant ministers, for example, have the courage to preach on the Trinity even on Trinity Sunday? They know in advance that parishioners will not readily follow their feeble efforts to explain an article of faith that they themselves so poorly understand as a result of their prior seminary education. Yet Lonergan is certainly correct in thinking that the doctrine of the Trinity and the other articles of Christian faith should be logically consistent with one another and have a transcultural and transgenera-

---

[22] Bernard Lonergan, *The Way to Nicea: The Dialectical Development of the Trinitarian Theology*, trans. Conn O'Donovan (Philadelphia: Westminster, 1976). This is an English translation of Lonergan's *De Deo Trino* (Rome: Gregorian University Press, 1964), 17–112.

[23] Ibid., 136.

tional plausibility. Otherwise, interpreting the doctrine of the Trinity in common sense language risks reducing it to a myth in the negative sense, something to be set aside as one comes of age.

But Lonergan may have overstated his case for the scientific approach to the dogma of the Trinity. His obvious assumption in *The Way to Nicea* is that there is only one true philosophical explanation of the doctrine of the Trinity that corresponds to the actual reality of the triune God. No reputable scientist, however, would ever make such a sweeping claim for his or her theory for the explanation of some aspect of physical reality. All scientific theories are subject to further testing in the light of new empirical evidence and should be revised or even rejected if evidence to the contrary is strong enough. A scientist can claim only that his theory represents the best available model for the explanation of the data here and now. In this respect Lonergan's assertion that the consubstantiality of the Son with the Father as defined by the Council of Nicaea represents a breakthrough in the scientific approach to the doctrine of the Trinity is overstated. De facto, it turned out to be a key factor in the medieval development of the doctrine of the Trinity, but this classical medieval model for the God-world relationship can and perhaps should be challenged in the light of contemporary human understanding of both God and the world, as we shall see in subsequent chapters.

Wolfhart Pannenberg

The last theologian whose work on the Trinity will be included in this chapter is Wolfhart Pannenberg, clearly one of the leading Protestant theologians of the second half of the twentieth century. In his multivolume *Systematic Theology* he first indicates where he both agrees and disagrees with Karl Barth on the relationship between divine revelation and human reason. In the end, only God can reveal Godself to human beings.[24] But human beings can come to some limited understanding of their ongoing need "to rise above the finitude of human existence to the thought of the infinite and the absolute," which can then later be identified with the God of biblical revelation.[25] Then, after reviewing the history of the Christian doctrine of the Trinity from the early church fathers through the Middle Ages and into the modern era, Pannenberg finally at the end

---

[24] Wolfhart Pannenberg, *Systematic Theology*, vol. 1, trans. Geoffrey Bromiley (Grand Rapids, MI: Eerdmans, 1991), 94.
[25] Ibid., 106.

of volume 1 sets forth his own trinitarian theology based on what he calls the "reciprocal self-distinction of Father, Son, and Spirit," both within the divine life and in salvation history.[26]

Here the key factor is the Lordship of the Father over creation as a result of the mission of the Son and the Spirit in salvation history: "As Jesus glorifies the Father and not himself, and precisely in so doing shows himself to be the Son of the Father, so the Spirit glorifies not himself but the Son, and in him the Father."[27] But in this way the Lordship, and in a qualified sense the deity of the Father, depends upon the acknowledgment of his Lordship both by the Son and the Spirit within the divine life and in the success of their mission to the world in the temporal order.[28] As Pannenberg comments, the world as the object of the Father's lordship "might not be necessary to his deity, since its existence owes its origin to his creative freedom, but the existence of a world is not compatible with his deity apart from his lordship over it. Hence, lordship goes hand in hand with the deity of God."[29] Thus, if God creates a world, then that world must eventually submit to God's lordship over it. The mission of Christ and the Spirit is to bring about this kingdom of God on earth.

This might well seem to imply something like predestination on Pannenberg's part, but he avoids that conclusion with his reflections on the relationship between time and eternity. Eternity is neither the negation of time (as the Greek philosopher Plato believed) nor simply unending time, time without beginning or end. Rather, eternity, as Boethius realized (see chap. 2), is the "simultaneous and perfect presence of unlimited life."[30] We human beings, for example, experience time as an ongoing succession of moments; thus we always see the future as in front of us and outside our ability to control and organize perfectly. For the three divine persons, on the contrary, eternity is likewise an experience of ongoing movement out of the past into the present and thence into the future, but it is a movement that they grasp in its fullness all at once as the "simultaneous and perfect presence of unlimited life." Hence, the future is not unknown to them as it is to us. The three divine persons

---

[26] Ibid., 308–19.

[27] Ibid., 315.

[28] Ibid., 324.

[29] Ibid., 313.

[30] Ibid., 404. Reference is to Boethius, *On the Consolation of Philosophy*, Bk. 5, chap. 6, n. 4.

already know how the world will come to an end even though they leave to us their creatures the actual decisions that over time will change the course of history and eventually bring about the end of the world. They stay involved with us, however, by using that higher knowledge of past, present, and future to prompt us to make the right decisions and thereby to assure a better world for ourselves and our posterity. What happens here and now, then, is our decision rather than theirs, but we have every reason to believe that the divine persons, given their unlimited knowledge of past, present, and future will find a way to bring cosmic history to a happy ending.[31]

Conclusion

In part 2 of this book, we will return to Pannenberg's understanding of the "reciprocal self-distinction" of the Father, Son, and Holy Spirit in virtue of their co-constitution of an all-embracing divine field of activity that in turn serves as the ontological ground or vital source of existence and activity for the world of creation. But for now we can bring part 1 to a close with a backward look at the preceding four chapters. We began with a brief review of the way in which the ancient Israelites struggled to affirm the existence of one God, Yahweh, in the midst of a pagan world worshiping multiple gods and goddesses. But with the life, death, and resurrection of Jesus everything changed for his Jewish followers. Without giving up belief in God as one, their experience of the risen Lord and of the Holy Spirit, above all in their celebration of the Eucharist, convinced them that God is triune, that there are three distinct "personalities" or centers of activity within the divine being, one of whom became incarnate in the person of Jesus. Then followed a lengthy period of reflection and testing of arguments in which various theories about the relations of the three divine persons to one another were actively debated. The challenge of Arius to the divinity of Jesus, in particular, provoked first the Council of Nicaea in 325 and then the First Council of Constantinople in 381 to hammer out doctrinal beliefs about the Trinity that

---

[31] See, however, Pannenberg, *Systematic Theology*, vol. 3, trans. Geoffrey W. Bromiley (Grand Rapids, MI: Eerdmans, 1998), 620, where he conjectures that those who even after death and the Last Judgment resist incorporation into the kingdom of God will be annihilated by the "fire of the divine glory." Hence, while he sets aside belief in hell as a place of unending torment for the damned, he does retain that belief under a new form, namely, nonexistence or annihilation.

would set the stage for the synthesizing activity of medieval theologians in both East and West. One unhappy consequence of this otherwise creative difference in approach to the doctrine of the Trinity on the part of both groups, however, was the breakup of the church in 1054 into separate Roman Catholic and Orthodox traditions.

In chapter 3 we noted how some medieval mystics and many early modern philosopher/scientists challenged the classical understanding of the Trinity worked out by Thomas Aquinas and other scholastic thinkers. A few of the mystics, such as Julian of Norwich and Theresa of Avila, added richness to the classical doctrine by their personal experiences of union with the divine persons. But other mystics, like the author of *The Cloud of Unknowing* and Meister Eckhart, appealed to a still deeper experience of total absorption into the divine ground of being. Furthermore, still another late medieval mystic, Nicholas of Cusa, laid the groundwork for the rise of scientific rationalism in the early modern period with his description of the physical universe as boundless in space and time and therefore governed by mathematical law. In the hands of philosopher/scientists like Descartes and Newton this became the basis for a new worldview in which God as Trinity was replaced by a unipersonal God who normally operated in the world through empirically established laws. This limited form of theism in turn led to deism, the belief that God had nothing to do with the world after the initial act of creation, and eventually to practical (if not theoretical) atheism, since religion and science were considered totally separate worlds of discourse.

In chapter 4, however, we saw how the doctrine of the Trinity underwent an amazing revival, spearheaded by Karl Barth's strong emphasis on the priority of the Divine Word to all forms of human reason. At the same time, with his focus on Jesus as the revealed Word of God, Barth laid the foundation for a deeper study of the way that the Trinity is active in salvation history. Eberhard Jüngel and Karl Rahner both emphasized the correspondence between the immanent Trinity, the inner life of God, and the economic Trinity, the Trinity as active in the world. On the one hand, this allowed for an innovative pastoral understanding of the doctrine of the Trinity at the hands of Catherine Mowry LaCugna. But, on the other hand, it raised new questions about the way the triune God is related to the world, questions that, as we shall see in part 2 of this book, are still being intensely debated today.

In brief, then, the doctrine of the Trinity has undergone a renaissance after a period of neglect in the early modern period. At the present time it has returned to center stage in the minds of many professional theologians since they recognize its importance for an integrated Christian worldview. While not quite the "hot topic" that it was for Christians at the time of the early councils of the church, it has regained its rightful place as the centerpiece of Christian life and worship in the modern world.

Part Two

New Critical Perspectives

Chapter Five

The Creative Suffering of God

As already noted in chapter 4, the twentieth century saw a strong revival of the doctrine of the Trinity, a revival inspired by the way that the three divine persons were seen as both collectively and individually at work in salvation history, our own daily lives. But implicit in this new linkage of the immanent Trinity and the economic Trinity is a question that unsettles many conservatively oriented Christians. Do the three divine persons suffer as a result of their involvement with us their creatures? If so, isn't this a denial of the classical understanding of God as immutable or unchanging? Furthermore, what's the point of God suffering with us? What we need is a God who can deliver us from the pain and suffering of this world, not simply "shed a tear" for us when bad things happen.

Karl Rahner avoided this issue by proposing that Jesus as the Incarnate Son of God suffered only in his human nature, not in the divine nature that he shared with the Father and the Spirit. So the Trinity as such would be immune from suffering even though one of its members would experience suffering and death as Jesus of Nazareth. But other theologians, beginning with Karl Barth, accepted the challenge of believing in the "passion" of God. In typical fashion, Barth argued that our human understanding of God derives from revelation, not from human reason. Thus, even though in terms of classical metaphysics God cannot suffer because God as perfect being is immutable, "from what God as man in Jesus Christ is, does and suffers we learn that 'God *can* do this.'"[1] Yet God

---

[1] Jüngel, *The Doctrine of the Trinity*, 85. Reference is to Karl Barth, *Church Dogmatics*, vol. IV/1, 187.

does not thereby forfeit his divinity but, rather, is "'in such a humiliation supremely alive,' so that 'he has actually maintained and revealed his deity precisely in the passion of this man as his eternal Son.'"[2]

Jürgen Moltmann: The Crucified God

Perhaps the most dramatic (and controversial) statement of the suffering of God as a result of involvement in this world, however, came from another distinguished German Protestant theologian, Jürgen Moltmann. In his book *The Crucified God*, Moltmann notes the "death of God" theology that preceded the publication of his own book and comments: "Jesus' death cannot be understood 'as the death of God', but only as death *in* God."[3] What is involved here is a change in relationship between God the Father, God the Son, and God the Holy Spirit in and through the passion, death, and resurrection of Jesus:

> To understand what happened between Jesus and his God and Father on the cross, it is necessary to talk in trinitarian terms. The Son suffers dying, the Father suffers the death of the Son. The grief of the Father here is just as important as the death of the Son. The Fatherlessness of the Son is matched by the Sonlessness of the Father, and if God has constituted himself as the Father of Jesus, then he also suffers the death of his Fatherhood in the death of the Son.[4]

Yet in their mutual surrender of Fatherhood and Sonship, the Father and the Son are reunited in the Holy Spirit as "the unconditioned and therefore boundless love which proceeds from the grief of the Father and the dying of the Son and reaches forsaken men [sic] in order to create in them the possibility and the force of new life."[5]

All this might seem like pure melodrama on Moltmann's part. But he is dead serious, because in his view Christian belief in the possibility of salvation for suffering human beings is otherwise impossible:

> Only if all disaster, forsakenness by God, absolute death, the infinite curse of damnation and sinking into nothingness is in God himself,

---

[2] Ibid., 87; Barth, *Church Dogmatics*, IV/1, 246–47.

[3] Jürgen Moltmann, *The Crucified God: The Cross of Christ as the Foundation and Criticism of Christian Theology*, trans. R. A. Wilson and John Bowden (New York: Harper & Row, 1974), 207.

[4] Ibid., 243.

[5] Ibid., 245.

is community with this God eternal salvation, infinite joy, indestructible election and divine life. The "bifurcation" in God must contain the whole uproar of history within it. . . . All human history, however much it may be determined by guilt and death, is taken up into this "history of God," i.e., into the Trinity, and integrated into the future of the "history of God."[6]

Moltmann is distinguishing here between the notion of "God in history," which leads only to unproductive debate between theists and atheists about the logical possibility of divine involvement in human history, and "history in God," which, as he sees it, opens up the biblical expectation of new creation and the transformation of this world through integration into the divine life.

As we have seen already in chapter 4 with the work of Catherine Mowry LaCugna, and as we will see later in this chapter with the God-world relationship presupposed by Alfred North Whitehead and most process theologians, there is a danger in theoretically incorporating salvation history into the "history of God" without further qualification. The result can be an unintended form of pantheism where God and the world are totally interdependent within an overarching cosmic process with a consequent loss of freedom on both sides. In a later work, *The Trinity and the Kingdom*, Moltmann consciously addresses this issue. That is, he reinterprets the classical doctrines of creation, redemption, and the transfiguration of the world in terms of an ongoing cosmic process in which the divine persons are intimately involved with their creatures without blurring the distinction between the divine and the human. Moltmann pictures creation, for example, as taking place within God by an act of divine self-withdrawal in order to let creation have "space" for itself within the divine being.[7] Yet from eternity "God has desired not only himself but the world too, for he did not merely want to communicate himself to himself; he wanted to communicate himself to the one who is other than himself. This is why the idea of the world is already inherent in the Father's love for the Son."[8] With reference to the doctrine of the redemption, Moltmann claims that the Son of God became human primarily, not to redeem us from our sins, but to share the divine life

---

[6] Ibid., 246.

[7] Jürgen Moltmann, *The Trinity and the Kingdom: The Doctrine of God*, trans. Margaret Kohl (San Francisco: Harper & Row, 1981), 109. Moltmann is making reference here to the doctrine of *zimsum* within Jewish mysticism, specifically the work of Isaac Luria.

[8] Ibid., 108.

with us. As a result, the incarnation of the Son "is neither a matter of indifference for God nor is it necessary for his divinity. If God is love, then . . . it is part of his loving self-communication and a matter of course for him to communicate himself, not only to his 'like' but also to his 'other.' It is only in and through its Other that love becomes *creative love*."[9] Finally, "in the transfiguration of the world through the Spirit all men [sic] turn to God and, moved by the Spirit, come to the Father through Christ the Son. In the glorification of the Spirit, world and times, people and things are gathered to the Father to become *his world*."[10]

Moltmann's vision of the interconnection between the Trinity and the kingdom of God on earth is truly inspirational. What is still missing, however, is a more precise philosophical explanation of how the three divine persons and all their creatures can thus coexist as both interdependent and independent of one another at the same time. The same problem, as I see it, exists for Whitehead and most process theologians. Whitehead, for example, in *Process and Reality* proposes: "God and the World are the contrasted opposites in terms of which Creativity achieves its supreme task of transforming disjoined multiplicity, with its diversities in opposition, into concrescent unity, with its diversities in contrast."[11] For Whitehead, accordingly, God and the world are implicated in one and the same cosmic process. Both are governed by what he calls Creativity, or the principle of creative advance into novelty within this world, and both God and the world can experience one another through participation in the same cosmic process. But can the necessary distinction between God and the world be thus maintained? Before addressing that question, we should take a closer look at Whitehead's overall philosophical scheme.

Whitehead's Worldview

Whitehead's basic presupposition is that momentary subjects of experience (what he calls "actual entities") are "the final real things of which the world is made up."[12] Even God is an "actual entity," although

---

9 Ibid., 117.

10 Ibid., 127.

11 Alfred North Whitehead, *Process and Reality: An Essay in Cosmology*, corrected edition, eds. Donald W. Sherburne and David Ray Griffin (New York: Free Press, 1978), 348.

12 Ibid., 18.

unlike us God is an eternal, fully infinite subject of experience. But, you may object, while human beings are clearly subjects of experience, there are a lot of "things" in this world that are just as clearly not subjects of experience (e.g., tables, chairs, all the inanimate objects of the material world). Whitehead, however, argues that, if all the things of this world are made up of atoms, what is an atom? Is it a tiny bit of inert matter or is it a momentary, self-constituting subject of experience, something that can bring itself into being by responding to what is going on around it? Scientists, for example, follow Albert Einstein in proposing that matter and energy are convertible. All that Whitehead is claiming is that energy has a psychic instead of a purely material base. That is, the energy measured by scientists comes from the ongoing interplay of momentary, self-constituting subjects of experience that aggregate into "societies," the persons and things of common sense experience.[13] Admittedly, we human beings cannot see and touch these "actual entities" as we look around us but we do have direct experience of actual entities in one area of life, namely, within our own consciousness. For as time passes we have different thoughts and feelings in response to what is happening all around us. We feel ourselves changing from moment to moment. Whitehead says that this is a perfect example of an ongoing society of actual entities and that we should think of everyone and everything else as likewise made up of actual entities (spiritual atoms) in dynamic interrelation.

All this may seem quite strange, even bizarre, until we realize how with such a scheme Whitehead can readily explain how God experiences the world and responds to it at every moment, and how all creatures, but above all we human beings, can likewise experience the presence and activity of God in our lives and respond to it, either positively or negatively. As Whitehead sees it, God mentally grasps or "prehends" everything that is going on in the world of creation, feels the feelings of every creature in its momentary self-constitution and then integrates all this empirical data into God's own ongoing self-constitution, what Whitehead calls the divine consequent nature.[14] Then, in virtue of the other dimension of the divine being, what Whitehead calls the primordial nature of God, God's comprehensive vision of possibilities for the world,[15] God can offer the next set of created actual entities an "initial aim" to

---

[13] Ibid., 34–35.
[14] Ibid., 346.
[15] Ibid., 343–44.

guide their processes of self-constitution.[16] Thus there is a back-and-forth relation between God as the transcendent actual entity and the ongoing succession of created actual entities which, gathered into "societies," make up the persons and things of our world from moment to moment. God feels the world in all its complex particularity, and the world of creatures feels the presence and activity of God at every moment in terms of divine initial aims directed at individual actual entities in their momentary processes of self-constitution.

Paul Fiddes: The Creative Suffering of God

In this way, God clearly is affected by what happens in this world and in that sense "suffers" with us in the "ups and downs" of life in this world. But, as Paul Fiddes comments, God's suffering is not purely passive, so that God is helpless to assist us in our suffering, but active or creative: "[W]hen God chooses to make our suffering his own he is subject to suffering but not subjected by it; he is under constraint from suffering, but it has no power to overwhelm him because he has freely chosen it as part of his own being. He triumphs over suffering because he chooses it for a purpose."[17] But why does God thus choose to suffer if God could eliminate suffering in this world simply by an exercise of divine power? Here Whitehead and Fiddes have a surprising answer. The real power of God is the power of persuasion, not coercion. To eliminate suffering through coercion, an exercise of omnipotence on God's part, is less divine than to eliminate suffering gradually through persuasion, that is, lovingly and compassionately urging us to change our harmful behavior patterns.

As already noted, in Whitehead's scheme God sends to each created actual entity or momentary subject of experience, an initial aim to guide it in its self-constitution. But that same created actual entity can refuse to accept the divine initial aim or can alter it in such a way that the aim no longer corresponds to what God had in mind for it. In this way, pain and suffering can come about both for the individual actual entity, the "society" to which it belongs, and for all the other "societies" of actual entities in its environment. But God keeps sending new initial aims to subsequent actual entities, new moments of experience for ourselves and everything else in this world, in order to correct, if possible, the evil

---

[16] Ibid., 244.
[17] Paul S. Fiddes, *The Creative Suffering of God* (Oxford: Clarendon Press, 1988), 62.

already done. Yet God is powerless to force such a change for the better since God is exclusively a God of persuasion, not a God of coercion.

Fiddes also argues that God operates in this world in a gentle, non-violent way. Pointing to the gospel narrative, he notes how the story of Jesus' passion, death, and resurrection can give new meaning and value to our own suffering *if* we choose to accept it.[18] This is not to deny that Jesus died feeling forsaken by his heavenly Father, as Moltmann has made clear. But the Father's personal involvement in the apparently senseless death of his Son encourages us to trust in divine providence and persuades us to be compassionate toward others as the Father has evidently cared for us in and through the person of his Son. Likewise, Fiddes sees the value of Whitehead's concept of the divine initial aim. For in feeling God's feelings for us in terms of the divine initial aim, we are not only consoled by God but given divine direction in dealing creatively with our own suffering and the suffering of others.[19]

The key to reconciliation with God, then, is what Fiddes calls "the creative journey of forgiveness," the slow and patient way in which God continues to offer us forgiveness through both the Gospel message and divine initial aims even though we initially are hesitant about, even hostile to, the divine offer of forgiveness.[20] We apprehend God as one who is shaped by the experience of the cross: "A suffering God who was and is always willing to forgive gains through the cross a new experience of the human condition that gives him access into our resistant hearts. He suffers changes in order to change us."[21] God is not internally changed in thus dealing with us; only God's style of approach to us is different in virtue of the experience of the suffering and death of his Son on the cross. In effect, God fulfills God's own being through self-giving love to all creatures much as we human beings experience self-transcendence in giving unselfishly to others.[22]

Yet Fiddes still has certain reservations about Whitehead's overall understanding of the God-world relationship: "Process thought, then, points in a valuable way to the powerful effect which an exchange of feelings between us and a suffering God can have upon us, but I believe that this insight can be carried through better with the more thoroughgoing

---

[18] Ibid., 144–52.
[19] Ibid., 152–57.
[20] Ibid., 157–69.
[21] Ibid., 167.
[22] Ibid., 169–73.

personal analogy for God which is offered by Trinitarianism."[23] I would certainly agree with Fiddes on this point. It is not the unipersonal God of Whitehead's metaphysics but the trinitarian God of the classical tradition that is needed for understanding how God can be involved in human suffering without undercutting God's transcendence to the world of creation. Otherwise, as noted above (p. 62) in the citation from *Process and Reality*, God and the world seem to be absorbed into one and the same cosmic process with God needing the world as much as the world needs God. If we are to avoid pantheism, a trinitarian understanding of the God-world relationship seems indispensable. Only thus can we be sure that the difference between God and the world is fully respected. But how is this to be done without sacrificing God's ability to suffer with creation as proposed by Moltmann, Fiddes, and Whitehead?

Making Space for One Another: A New Approach to Intersubjectivity

Let us begin by looking at what happens between two human beings in close contact with one another, for basically the same problem seems to be present. How can I share in your life and you share in my life, in effect, create a common life in which we remain ourselves but are changed, personally enriched, through ongoing relation to one another? Martin Buber in his classic work *I and Thou* talked about the experience of the "between" when I treat you as a Thou and you treat me as a Thou.[24] We create a common "space" for our relationship, which allows us to feel in close contact with one another and yet allows us to keep a certain distance from one another at the same time. Unfortunately, Buber did not elaborate on this somewhat mysterious notion of the "between," beyond noting how important it was for true interpersonal relations. But as I see it, there is a way to make it intelligible through a modest rethinking of one of Whitehead's key categories, the notion of "society."

Recall that Whitehead described "societies" as aggregates of actual entities (momentary subjects of experience). There are different aggregates of these actual entities corresponding to the different persons and things of common sense experience because each aggregate has a different pattern of organization or self-constitution for its member actual

[23] Ibid., 157.
[24] See Martin Buber, *I and Thou*, trans. Roland Gregor Smith (New York: Scribner's, 1970), 37–72.

entities, what Whitehead calls a "common element of form."[25] Yet if these aggregates of actual entities last only as long as the actual entities here and now making them up, then the societies of actual entities likewise last only for an instant and must be replaced by a new set of actual entities and a new society in the next moment. The felt continuity of existence and activity that we perceive in ourselves and the persons and things around us thus seems to be lost. Whitehead, however, was insistent that what actually endures over time is simply the "common element of form," the basic pattern of existence and activity for a society of actual entities. We may think that we are the same person from one moment to another. But in point of fact we are a new person at each moment, even though we find ourselves acting the same way, having basically the same pattern of behavior, as in the past.

Common Space:
Where Separate Fields of Activity Overlap and Intermingle

But this still seems like a poor excuse for our strong sense of self-identity from moment to moment. It is not just the pattern of our lives but we ourselves as human beings that somehow survive from moment to moment. There is, however, another explanation for our sense of enduring self-identity within the context of Whitehead's philosophy, if we are willing to reinterpret some of Whitehead's own beliefs about these societies of actual entities. For he also spoke of "societies" as "environments" for any given set of actual entities.[26] The word "environment" suggests that Whiteheadian societies might be considered enduring fields of activity for ever-new sets of actual entities. In this way, the actual entities can come and go at every instant; but the fields endure, structured by the way these actual entities relate to one another from moment to moment. If Whiteheadian societies are understood this way, then what is our mind but an enduring field of activity over which we preside in successive moments of consciousness? What is our body but a complex set of fields of activity corresponding to what is organically taking place inside our body all the time (heart pumping and blood circulating, lungs breathing, stomach and intestines digesting food, etc.)? Finally, what are all the persons and things around us but co-participants with us in an

[25] Whitehead, *Process and Reality*, 34.
[26] Ibid., 90.

all-embracing field of activity wherein we all live, move, and have our being?

Yet does it really help to think of ourselves, other people, and the entire world in this way, namely, as interrelated fields of activity for subjects of experience in dynamic interaction? Recall what we said earlier about creating a "between," a space between ourselves and others so that we can have a common life and yet be ourselves at the same time. If I as an individual human being have my own space (personal field of activity) but can make contact with other people and external things in different spaces, we can together over time create a common space, build a community. I keep my space; you keep yours. Yet in the space between us we can set up patterns of interaction that last over time. The larger the community of persons and things thus involved, of course, the more stable the patterns of interaction. In living and working together, for example, people establish a given way of life, set up businesses, found schools for the education of their children, and so forth. They fill in the common space between them with visible institutions and with invisible but still tangible, commonly accepted ways of dealing with one another.

Conclusion

In the next chapter we will take up again this field-oriented approach to our life together and see how it fits into what has been called the "social" model of the Trinity. But even now we can see how this new way of looking at reality can solve the problem of how God can suffer with us and still be God. For, given this model of the God-world relationship, we share the same "space" with the three divine persons, experience their presence and activity in our lives even as they share the ups and downs of human life with us. Call it, if you will, the kingdom of God on earth. In any case the three divine persons share our pain and we in some measure feel their presence and activity in our lives, experience their suffering in dealing with us at every moment. Yet no one is overwhelmed by the experience. The three divine persons continue to live their life and we live ours even as we share common concerns, feel one another's pain and suffering.

Chapter Six

The Problem of the One and the Many

Some years ago the celebrated English theologian Colin Gunton wrote a book with the intriguing title *The One, the Three and the Many: God, Creation and the Culture of Modernity*. In his view, much of what is wrong with the modern world can be traced to a mistaken notion of the relationship between the One and the Many, and the way to remedy this mistake is through a return to the classical Greek understanding of the doctrine of the Trinity as *perichoresis*, the moving in and out, or dancing around, of the divine persons in their ongoing relations to one another. Before dismissing this as a ridiculous oversimplification of contemporary social problems, let's summarize his argument in the next few paragraphs.

The Trinity as Model for Contemporary Life

Gunton claims that modern life is full of paradoxes; we live in an era "which has sought freedom and bred totalitarianism; which has taught us our insignificance in the vastness of the universe, and yet sought to play god with that same universe; which has sought to control the world, and yet let loose forces that may destroy the earth."[1] This has happened because we no longer have a strong sense either of personal identity or of corporate unity. We feel "disengaged" from one another, inclined to use one another "as a mere means for realizing our will, and not as in

---

[1] Colin E. Gunton, *The One, the Three and the Many: God, Creation and the Culture of Modernity* (Cambridge University Press, 1993), 13.

some way integral to our being."[2] What we need instead is a renewed sense of relationality, the right kind of engagement with the other "that gives due weight to both one and many, to both particular and universal, to both otherness and relation."[3]

Terrorism, for example, in one form or another has become an all-too-common feature of human life around the world. But are not terrorist tactics sometimes a form of protest by subordinate ethnic groups against what they regard as suppression of their own goals and values by an insensitive majority or, in any case, by the homogenizing tendencies of the mainstream culture? People thus seek to uphold their own race, culture, and religion by force rather than through dialogue and communication, since such efforts at consensus and mutual agreement seem in their eyes doomed to fail from the start. Even among those who constitute the majority group within a given society, there is an implicit tendency among its members to conform to a single dominant pattern of thought and behavior, to fit into a basically uniform approach to life, while at the same time many individuals in the group continue to insist on the freedom to be themselves, to follow their own personal needs and desires.

Where else, says Gunton, should Christians look for guidance in overcoming this dichotomy between the One and the Many, universality and particularity, in modern life but through reflection on the doctrine of the Trinity, "a conception of God who is both one and three, whose being consists in a relationality that derives from the otherness-in-relation of Father, Son and Spirit"?[4] The problem, of course, is that the classical formulation of the Trinity in both East and West, as we have already seen in chapters 1 and 2, was itself in large part infected by a mistaken understanding of the relation between the One and the Many. Theologians in the West so emphasized the unity of the divine nature over the plurality of the persons that they were in danger of falling into the heresy of modalism, one God with three different historical appearances or manifestations. Theologians in the East, on the contrary, so emphasized the plurality of the persons over the unity of the divine nature that they were prone to either tritheism (belief in three gods) or subordinationism (the Father somehow being considered more divine than either the Son or the Holy Spirit).

[2] Ibid., 14.
[3] Ibid., 6–7.
[4] Ibid., 7.

Yet, says Gunton, properly reinterpreted, the notion of the triune God should be able to provide an example of unity-in-plurality for human beings in their dealings with one another. The triune God, after all, as creator of heaven and earth "writes plurality into the being of things."[5] Every individual entity is unique in God's eyes. But the same triune God also sees the world as a universe, an interconnected and coordinated whole. So if the divine persons have no trouble with the problem of the One and the Many, either in their relations with one another or in their dealings with us their creatures, maybe we should rethink what we mean when we say that God is three-in-one, a Trinity. Does the notion of the Trinity provide us with an unexpected way to solve the problem of the One and the Many, above all, in our dealings with one another in the contemporary world?

New Ideals for Modern Life in Community

Gunton says yes; his strategy is to rethink the medieval transcendental ideals of Being (Unity, Truth, Goodness, and Beauty) because in their original formulation they apply only to individuals in isolation. That is, according to classical metaphysics, everything within the world of creation has its own unity, truth, goodness, and beauty quite apart from its relation to anything else. Instead, Gunton proposes what are for him a far more important set of transcendental ideals that apply to the workings of communities and environments within creation. These new transcendental ideals, says Gunton, are exemplified in the pattern of existence and activity for the three divine persons in their ongoing relations with one another.

The first such transcendental ideal is *perichoresis*, the dynamic unity in plurality of the divine persons within their communitarian life. Applied to the world of creation, this transcendental ideal means that everything in the world is dependent on everything else; everything "contributes to the being of everything else, enabling everything to be what it distinctively is."[6] The second transcendental ideal is particularity or substantiality. Each person or thing in this world is unique in its individual identity. Yet it is constituted in its particularity not by what it is in itself apart from other entities but by what it is in terms of its relation to other things: "Something is real—what it is and not another thing—by virtue

---

[5] Ibid., 151.
[6] Ibid., 166.

of the way that it is held in being not only by God but also by other things in the particular configurations of space and time in which its being is constituted; that is to say, in its createdness."[7] In other words, I am what I am only because of what you are both in yourself and in relationship to me. The third and last transcendental ideal is relationality or, at the level of human interaction, sociality. Sociality implies a pattern of mutual giving and receiving whereby human beings achieve self-fulfillment and true self-identity through giving themselves in unselfish love to one another.[8]

If these three transcendental ideals that are prefigured in the Christian doctrine of the Trinity could be implemented within the world of creation, then there would no longer be a problem of the One and the Many, the reconciliation of universality and particularity among human beings in terms of race, culture, and religion. Unity would be based upon the recognition and acceptance of particularity among the peoples of the world. Differences would enrich rather than antagonize those engaged in ongoing interaction with one another; genuine mutual understanding would become possible on different levels of communication (political, economic, cultural, religious). The goal of community life among individuals would not be bland uniformity in thought and practice, but dynamic, ever-changing unity-in-difference after the model of the persons of the Trinity in their ongoing relations to one another.

Jürgen Moltmann: The Social Model of the Trinity

Given these thought-provoking remarks from Gunton, we can now take up the so-called social model of the Trinity, the image of God as a functioning community of divine persons. This model of God has grown in popularity in recent years but is still opposed, or at least held in suspicion, by many contemporary theologians who think it subtly undermines traditional belief in God as one. Perhaps in some cases they are right. Jürgen Moltmann, for example, whose theory on suffering in God we reviewed in the last chapter, is a firm believer in the Trinity as a communion of divine persons. But he may have overstated his case in claiming that monotheism, belief in God as one, is actually a betrayal of the true Christian understanding of God.[9] As Moltmann sees it, God is

---

[7] Ibid., 200.

[8] Ibid., 227.

[9] Moltmann, *The Trinity and the Kingdom: The Doctrine of God*, trans. Margaret Kohl (San Francisco: Harper & Row, 1981), 10–20.

neither a transcendent individual entity (Pure Act of Being), as Aquinas presupposed in setting forth Five Ways for proving the existence of God in his *Summa Theologiae*,[10] nor a transcendent individual Ego (subject of activity), as the German philosopher Hegel and later Barth proposed.[11] Rather, in line with the New Testament, God is the dynamic union of three divine subjects of activity within a unique community of pure self-giving love: "We understand the scriptures as the testimony to the history of the Trinity's relations of fellowship, which are open to men and women, and open to the world. This trinitarian hermeneutics leads us to think in terms of relationships and communities" not only within God but also everywhere in the world of creation.[12]

The social model of the Trinity, as Moltmann here presents it, thus clearly represents a new way of thinking about the world as well as about God. But it still awakens anxiety in other Christian theologians that the precious heritage of belief in one God that Christians share with Jews and Muslims has thereby been lost. One has inadvertently capitulated to tritheism, belief in three gods who admittedly work together well in dealing with creation but who are separate from one another in their individual existence and activity. In effect, then, the three-in-one have to be more one than three or polytheism results. But in defense of Moltmann's position, we can ask with Colin Gunton whether or not our deep-rooted misgivings about tritheism are to be traced to an implicit misunderstanding of the relationship between the One and the Many.

That is, if we believe that the One is itself an individual entity or substance, then the One and the Many cannot simultaneously coexist. Either the Many are absorbed into the higher-order unity of the One as its component parts or members, or the independent existence of the One is an illusion since upon closer inspection the One is nothing more than an aggregate of separate substances. Yet, if on the contrary we believe that the One is not an entity or a substance but a unifying activity, a *perichoresis* among its members as seen in the way that Gunton and Moltmann explain the doctrine of the Trinity, then the Many and the One can simultaneously coexist. The Many are together a new kind of One,

---

[10] Ibid., 11–12. See, however, Thomas Aquinas, *Summa Theologiae*, I, question 2, art. 3. See also I, question 3, art. 5, where Aquinas explicitly repudiates the idea that God is a substance, even the supreme substance. Since God is unique, God cannot be described by any logical category likewise applicable to creatures. But Moltmann, in my judgment, was still correct in saying that the Five Ways point to the nature of God as Subsistent Being (*Ipsum Esse Subsistens*), not the personal reality of God.

[11] Moltmann, *The Trinity and the Kingdom*, 17–18.

[12] Ibid., 19.

a corporate reality rather than a higher-order individual entity. The unity thus achieved is the unity of an ongoing community of persons, an all-encompassing environment of persons and things together.

Everything thus depends upon one's prior understanding of the relationship of the One and the Many, and likewise upon one's implicit understanding of the nature of God. If God is conceived as a single person or an individual entity, then the world of creation will likewise be seen as made up of individual entities that are related to one another in various ways but still basically separate from one another. But if God is conceived as a social or corporate reality, namely, as a community of divine persons, then the world of creation becomes easy to picture as a mega-community, a systematically ordered set of subcommunities. Nothing in creation, then, exists simply on its own. Every individual person or thing is part of some kind of community, and that community in turn is part of an even bigger environment. In the end, the entire world is one big community, an all-encompassing environment for everything going on inside of it. So much thus depends upon how one pictures God, since by definition creation is made in the image of God its Creator.

Leonardo Boff: The Trinity as Model for Social Change

Still another contemporary theologian who has used the social model for the doctrine of the Trinity is Leonardo Boff, a Brazilian theologian well known for his books on liberation theology and environmental theology. In two books published a year apart, first *Trinity and Society* and then *Holy Trinity, Perfect Community*, Boff indicates how the model of the Trinity as a communion of divine persons is very useful as an ideal for poor people around the world in their struggle to overcome exploitation by the rich and powerful in their midst. Working with the model of the Trinity as a perfect community, poor people can resist the negative impact on themselves of both liberal capitalism and socialism. Liberal-capitalist society, for example, "means the dictatorship of the property-owning classes with their individualistic and business interests always shored up by mechanisms of state control."[13] The rich, in other words, find a way legally to exploit the poor. Societies with a socialist regime, to be sure, "are founded on a right principle, that of communion between

---

[13] Leonardo Boff, *Trinity and Society*, trans. Paul Burns (Maryknoll, NY: Orbis, 1988), 149.

all and the involvement of all in the means of production."[14] But socialist regimes tend to be heavy-handed in their insistence on uniformity without regard for real differences between persons and groups within the state. Within the Trinity, however, "there is no domination by one side, but convergence of the Three in mutual acceptance and giving. . . . Therefore, a society that takes its inspiration from trinitarian communion cannot tolerate class differences, dominations based on power (economic, sexual or ideological) that subjects those who are different to those who exercise that power."[15]

In another book published ten years later, Boff used the social model of the Trinity to organize his approach to ecology and the environment:

> Ecological discourse is structured around the web of relationships, interdependencies, and inclusions that sustain and constitute our universe. Together with unity (a single cosmos, a single planet Earth, a single human species, and so forth) diversity also flourishes (galaxy clusters, solar systems, biodiversity, and multiplicity of races, cultures and individuals). This co-existence between unity and diversity opens an area where we may consider our understanding of divinity in terms of trinity and communion.[16]

The three divine persons are one God, not three gods, because of their dynamic interrelatedness; they have no existence apart from one another. In similar fashion, everything in this world is dynamically interrelated with everything else. Moreover, recognition of this fact is the indispensable starting point for human efforts to improve the environment and to sustain an ecologically balanced world order.

Ted Peters, while acknowledging the contribution of Boff to both liberation theology and environmental theology, nevertheless sees inconsistencies in Boff's use of the social model for the Trinity. For Boff continues to affirm the so-called relationships of origin within the classical model of the Trinity. That is, he continues to regard the Father as the First Person within the Trinity and thus as the source of life and love for the Son and the Holy Spirit. But this implies that in some sense the Son and the Holy Spirit are subordinate to the Father, not the Father's equal within

---

[14] Ibid., 150.

[15] Ibid., 151. See also Leonardo Boff, *Holy Trinity, Perfect Community*, trans. Phillip Berryman (Maryknoll, NY: Orbis, 2000), 63–67.

[16] Leonardo Boff, *Cry of the Earth, Cry of the Poor*, trans. Phillip Berryman (Maryknoll, NY: Orbis, 1997), 154–55.

the Trinity as logically demanded by the notion of *perichoresis*.[17] Peters is certainly correct that there is a tension between relationships of origin and relationships of equality among the divine persons, something that has existed since the original formulation of *perichoresis* by St. John Damascene and the other Greek fathers of the church (see chap. 2).

But what Peters overlooks is that Boff is consciously moving away from the traditional understanding of cause and effect within classical metaphysics, in which the cause always preexists the effect, to a "processive and dynamic metaphysics," in which cause and effect come into existence at the same time and are mutually interdependent.[18] In this way neither the cause nor the effect can exist apart from the other; neither has priority over the other. Applied to the doctrine of the Trinity, this means:

> God is a Trinity of persons intertwined in love and communion. The three have their origin from all eternity, none being anterior to the others. . . . If this is so, it follows that everything in God is triadic [involving all three divine persons]; everything is *Patreque, Filioque* and *Spirituque*."[19]

Thus Boff consciously sets aside the accusation of subordinationism among the divine persons or of tritheism (belief in three gods) since these terms are simply the relic of an outdated metaphysics. Within a "dynamic processive metaphysics," on the contrary, in which the Many are dynamically interrelated so as to constitute the higher-order unity of the One as a specifically social reality, subordinationism and tritheism no longer make any sense.

Wolfhart Pannenberg: Spirit as Force-Field and Person

Another theologian who successfully combines the classical relationships of origin among the divine persons with the notion of *perichoresis*

---

[17] Peters, *God as Trinity*, 113. See also Boff, *Trinity and Society*, 139–40.

[18] Boff, *Trinity and Society*, 141–42, 145–46.

[19] Ibid., 146. NB: The Latin phrase at the end is translated as "[from] both the Father, and the Son, and the Holy Spirit." Boff is here rephrasing one of the key points at issue from the dispute between the Western and the Eastern Orthodox churches about the eternal procession of the Holy Spirit within the divine life (see chap. 2) so as to claim that each divine person is co-responsible for their ongoing threefold self-constitution as one God.

or the basic coequality of the persons within the divine life is Wolfhart Pannenberg. As we have seen already in chapter 4, Pannenberg lays heavy stress on the Lordship of the Father and the submission of the Son, the Holy Spirit, and all of creation to the Lordship of the Father. But he also claims that the deity or the self-identity of the Father is thereby dependent upon the ongoing submission of the Son, the Holy Spirit and, with the act of creation, all creatures. Hence, the Lordship of the Father, first over the Son and the Spirit within the divine life and then over all of us within creation, is limited and controlled by our collective response. In a sense, the Father needs us for the exercise of Lordship over creation almost as much as we need the Father for our very existence. There is then an inescapable mutuality of relationship here which softens the otherwise autocratic understanding of Lordship taken by itself.

But Pannenberg also maintains the basic coequality of the divine persons with his creative rethinking of the notion of Spirit. In his view, the word "Spirit" refers not only to the Holy Spirit as one of the divine persons but also to the underlying nature of God, that which enables all three divine persons to coexist in dynamic interrelation. "Spirit," in other words, is not to be understood as Mind, presumably the Mind of the Father as the ultimate source of the divine life, but as breath or wind, as in numerous passages in the Old and New Testament (e.g., the Spirit of God moving over the primeval waters in Gen 1:1; the Spirit of God reanimating the dry bones of the Israelites in Ezek 37:1-14; the Spirit of God descending upon the Apostles in the upper room at Pentecost in Acts 2:1-4). In such cases, says Pannenberg, "Spirit" refers to the underlying nature of God as a force or dynamism that empowers the three divine persons to set up a conjoint "force-field" for their dynamic interrelation.[20]

What he has in mind here is the notion of a force-field in theoretical physics that is organized and structured by the energy events taking place within it. Applied to the doctrine of the Trinity, this notion of the divine Spirit as a force-field yields intriguing results. The three divine persons, for example, are fully shaped by this power of love even as they each contribute in different ways to the force-field thereby set up. One could also claim that human communities are force-fields for the interaction of their members, but in human communities the members can find ways to resist the power of the field:

[20] Pannenberg, *Systematic Theology*, vol. 1, trans. Geoffrey Bromiley (Grand Rapids, MI: Eerdmans, 1991), 382.

> Even a number of human persons can be brought together in a living
> fellowship by a common spirit. In the human fellowship, of course,
> each individual can evade the common spirit. The person is basically
> independent of the spirit. The trinitarian persons, however, are not
> independent of the Spirit of love that binds them. They are simply
> manifestations and forms—eternal forms—of the one divine essence
> [the divine power of love].[21]

The three divine persons are thus interrelated centers of action for one
and the same divine life or force-field animated by the spirit of love. In
this way tritheism is avoided since the divine persons do not first exist
in themselves and then unite so to carry on the work of creation, redemption, and sanctification. They are three-in-one in their very being as God
even apart from creation because they cannot exist as individuals apart
from the field.[22]

There is a remarkable coincidence here between Pannenberg's understanding of the nature of God as a force-field for the coexistence of the
three divine persons and my own adaptation of Whitehead's notion of
"society" as a structured field of activity for its constituent actual entities
(see chap. 5). In both cases there is a presupposition that subjects of experience need space both to be themselves and to relate to other subjects
of experience through creation of a common space for their conjoint
existence and activity. As I indicated in chapter 5 and have developed
elsewhere,[23] this field metaphor for the interaction of subjects of experience opens up a new and unexpectedly productive way of looking at
the God-world relationship so that God and the world remain distinct
from one another and yet are always dynamically interrelated.

The Divine Matrix

That is, the three divine persons first co-constitute their own space,
what I have called "the divine matrix," for their conjoint existence and
activity. The world of creation then comes into existence within this

---

[21] Ibid., 383.

[22] Ibid., 385. See also 389: "The one God is the acting God, the subject of his action.
But this being as subject is not a fourth in God alongside the three persons of Father,
Son and Spirit. It does not precede the persons and find development in the trinitarian
differentiation. It expresses their living fellowship in action toward the world."

[23] See, e.g., Bracken, *The Divine Matrix: Creativity as Link between East and West*
(Maryknoll, NY: Orbis, 1995), 52–69; likewise, *The One in the Many: A Contemporary
Reconstruction of the God-World Relationship* (Grand Rapids, MI: Eerdmans, 2001),
109–30, 157–78.

divine matrix as a very large but still finite set of fields of activity for created actual entities or created subjects of experience. All creatures thus exist in God but still have their own space to be themselves and to relate both to one another and to the three divine persons within the common space that the New Testament calls the kingdom of God. In technical terms, this understanding of the God-world relationship is called panentheism (as opposed to pantheism): everything exists in God but has its own existence and activity distinct from God. God always remains the Creator and Sustainer of the world of creation since it came into existence by a free decision on the part of the divine persons and only continues to exist through ongoing finite participation in the divine life or divine community. But creation as a whole, and every creature within it, still has its own existence and activity distinct from God.

Many disciples of Whitehead, following the lead of Charles Hartshorne, picture God as the "soul" of the world and the world as the "body" of God.[24] This too is an example of panentheism, everything created existing in God and yet being independent of God. But in my judgment it is less suitable to describe the God-world relationship from a Christian perspective than the field-oriented approach sketched above. For if God is the "soul" of the world and the world is the "body" of God, then God seems to need the world for God's existence as much as the world needs God for its existence. Gone is the freedom of God to create or not to create, to create out of overflowing love for creatures rather than out of a personal need to be in charge of some world, even if not always of our world. Likewise, gone is our freedom as creatures of God to respond to God's "initial aims" in the way that we want. We become equivalently God's "body parts."

Conclusion

Not only Whiteheadians but also many other contemporary theologians are attracted to the soul-body metaphor to illustrate the God-world relationship. They see quite well, to be sure, the limitations of this model as an explanation of how God relates to the world and vice-versa. Yet they still hesitate to take the next step and think instead of God as a community of divine persons who incorporate all of creation into their own

---

[24] See, e.g., Charles Hartshorne, "The Compound Individual," in *Philosophical Essays for Alfred North Whitehead*, ed. F. S. C. Northrup (New York: Russell & Russell, 1936), 218–20; likewise by the same author, *Man's Vision of God and the Logic of Theism* (Hamden, CN: Archon Books, 1964), 174–211.

divine communitarian life.[25] Perhaps the fear of being accused of tritheism (belief in three gods) is still very strong even though, as this chapter should have made clear, the rival notions of tritheism and subordinationism among the divine persons rest upon an outdated metaphysics with too much emphasis on individual entities and with far too little attention paid to the communities or environments to which these individual entities inevitably belong.[26] In any event, we will return to this image of living within God, living within the divine field of activity and at the same time contributing to it by what we say and do, in subsequent chapters, above all, in chapter 9.

[25] See, e.g., Ian G. Barbour, *Religion in an Age of Science* (San Francisco: Harper & Row, 1990), 260: "We can think of God as *the leader of a cosmic community*. It is neither a monarchy nor a democracy, since one member is pre-eminent but not all-powerful . . . God's role is creative participation and persuasion in inspiring the community of beings toward new possibilities of a richer life together." Barbour thus thinks of the world as a cosmic community but holds back from claiming that the world as a mega-community is part of the divine community. See also by the same author *Religion and Science: Contemporary and Historical Issues* (San Francisco: HarperCollins, 1997), 331.

[26] See on this point William J. Hill, *The Three-Personed God: The Trinity as a Mystery of Salvation* (Washington, DC: Catholic University of America Press, 1982), 217–37, 268–72. Hill first surveys various theories on the Trinity as a divine community and finds many of them (my own theory included) as bordering on tritheism. Then in developing his own position on the immanent Trinity he concludes: "The persons in God thus constitute a divine intersubjectivity: Father, Son, and Spirit are three centers of consciousness in community, in mutual communication" (272). Yet, says Hill, this is not tritheism since they "are conscious by way of one essential consciousness," the consciousness of God as an individual entity. But if the essence or nature of God is to be a community, then the consciousness of God is necessarily a shared consciousness. Thus reality (even the reality of God) is essentially social; individuals exist only inasmuch as they participate in communities, environments, etc.

Chapter Seven

What's in a Name?

In the last two chapters we discussed various challenges to the classical formulation of the doctrine of the Trinity. In chapter 5, for example, we dealt with the possibility of the creative suffering of the divine persons in dealing with creation and thereby challenged the classical understanding of God as unchanging or immutable. In chapter 6 we explored the notion of *perichoresis* from the Greek fathers as it has been recently employed by Colin Gunton, Jürgen Moltmann and other contemporary theologians. As a result we found ourselves questioning the traditional fear of tritheism (belief in three gods) among trinitarian thinkers. But in both these cases the doctrine of the Trinity itself was never called into question. In the next two chapters, however, both the customary formulation of the doctrine and (at least with certain theologians) the doctrine itself, the very idea of the Trinity as a representation or symbol of the reality of God, is the subject of critical scrutiny. Has the doctrine of the Trinity over time become a stumbling block in better relations between Christian men and women? Is the Trinity an obstacle rather than a help to Christians engaged in interreligious dialogue, serious conversation with those belonging to other religions? We will address the first question in this chapter and save the second question for chapter 8.

The Origin of the Feminist Movement

Unquestionably one of the most significant and far-reaching social movements in Western society within the last 150 years has been the gradual growth in awareness (among both women and men) of the repressed status of women within traditional male-dominated civil society. It began, at least in the United States, with the suffrage movement, the right of women to vote. Elizabeth Cady Stanton, the early leader of the suffrage movement, was convinced in 1848 that the time had come for the "question of woman's wrongs to be laid before the public" by women themselves since "woman alone can understand the height, the depth, the length, and breadth of her own degradation."[1] Together with her chief collaborator, Susan B. Anthony, Stanton made some notable advances for women's rights by the time of her death in 1902. Within another generation, in 1920, an amendment to the United States Constitution was passed giving women the cherished right to vote. But then the women's movement seemed to lose energy, even disappear from the public eye. Only after World War II with the affirmation of women's rights in the Charter of the United Nations in 1945 and, above all, with the publication of *The Second Sex* by Simone de Beauvoir in 1949 was the stage set for a resurgence of interest in women's rights that has clearly gathered momentum with the passage of time. Today the women's movement, which started in 1848 with a meeting in a small town in upstate New York, has become truly international in its membership and global in its range of interests, addressing issues related to international politics, global economics, and preservation of the environment as well as the rights of women everywhere around the world.

Mary Daly: Sexism in the Roman Catholic Church

Within this chapter there is space to consider only a few representative figures within the Christian (or post-Christian) feminist movement who have made specific reference to the doctrine of the Trinity and/or the God-world relationship from a Christian perspective. Chief among these women writers, of course, is Mary Daly, who created quite a stir in theological circles, first with the publication of *The Church and the Second Sex* in 1968 and then five years later with *Beyond God the Father*. As the title of her first book implies, she initially wanted to critique and, if possible, to reform institutional structures and practices within the Catholic Church that have historically kept women in a subordinate

---

[1] As quoted by Miriam Schneir, introduction to *Feminism In Our Time: The Essential Writings, World War II to the Present*, ed. Miriam Schneir (New York: Random House, 1994), ix.

position. With respect to doctrinal issues, she simply noted that "warped notions of sexual relation and of woman may be the roots of weak and inadequate conceptions concerning God, Christ, revelation, the Church and the sacraments."[2]

In her second book, *Beyond God the Father*, Daly changed her focus and directly addressed doctrinal issues that prejudice the status of women in the church,[3] especially the doctrine of God the Father, the Genesis account of the fall of Adam and Eve, and redemption of the human race through Jesus as the Incarnate Word of God. In each of these areas she raises important criticisms of traditional church doctrine. For example, with reference to the image of God as Father or divine Patriarch, she notes: "If God in 'his' heaven is a father ruling 'his' people, then it is in the 'nature' of things and according to divine plan and the order of the universe that society be male-dominated."[4] Yet, argues Daly, simply naming God as "her" rather than "him" would be of limited value and in the end would be a trivialization of the problem of growth in personal maturity for women. Along the same lines, one could argue that treating God as male likewise jeopardizes what it means for men to become truly human. For men are thereby co-opted into the value system represented by the notion of patriarchy, the alleged inherent superiority of men over women, which effectively prevents them from getting in touch with the full range of human feelings and desires proper to becoming a mature human being.[5]

But if this be the case, what is to be done? Daly suggests that the word "God" be henceforth considered a verb instead of a noun, an activity rather than an individual entity: "Why indeed must 'God' be a noun? Why not a verb—the most active and dynamic of all? Hasn't the naming of 'God' as a noun been an act of murdering that dynamic Verb? And

[2] Mary Daly, *The Church and the Second Sex* (New York: Harper & Row, 1975), 188.

[3] In an autobiographical preface to the Harper Colophon edition of *The Church and the Second Sex* in 1975 and in a "feminist postchristian introduction" written at the same time, Daly makes clear her reservations about the book in its original format and indicates that she has moved from being a "radical Catholic" to being a "postchristian feminist."

[4] Mary Daly, *Beyond God the Father: Toward a Philosophy of Women's Liberation* (Boston, MA: Beacon Press, 1973), 13.

[5] Cf. on this point the German philosopher Hegel's celebrated analysis of the master-slave relation in his *Phenomenology of Mind*, part 2 (Self-Consciousness), trans. J. B. Baillie (New York: Harper Torchbook, 1967), 234–40. As Hegel makes clear, the master is ultimately less free than the slave and needs the slave to be liberated from the "slavery" of being always a master.

isn't the Verb infinitely more personal than a mere static noun?"[6] Daly points here to a key issue in the classical Christian understanding of God. But she may have overstated her case in thus logically opposing to one another verbs and nouns. Classical Christian theology admittedly preferred nouns to verbs in talking about God; she prefers verbs to nouns. But verbs and nouns would seem to be necessarily interconnected. Verbs need nouns to specify the subject of the activity represented by the verb. Nouns need verbs to escape purely "nominal" reality, being simply a name without further qualification.

Nonetheless, even with this caution Daly's proposal is very important since it forces us to reconsider something that has been more or less taken for granted in Western philosophy since the time of Plato and Aristotle, namely, the presupposition that activity follows upon being (*agere sequitur esse*). One must first exist and only then one can start to act. As Daly suggests, why not the reverse, namely, that being follows upon activity (*esse sequitur agere*)? Through persistently acting in a certain way, we gradually have become who we are right now. Becoming, therefore, is more characteristic of ourselves as individuals and of the world in which we live than Being. We and the world around us never stay the same for any length of time. Slowly but surely, everything is changing.

The great medieval theologian Thomas Aquinas was apparently on the verge of affirming this priority of Becoming over Being with his understanding of the doctrine of the Trinity (see chap. 2). That is, Aquinas claimed that the three divine persons are "subsistent relations," three very different but still dynamically interrelated ways of being the one God.[7] But, just as Daly claimed above, Aquinas seems to have understood the term "relation" more as a noun (as something linking one thing to another) than as a verb (as the actual activity of relating to another). So in Aquinas's theology of the Trinity the three divine persons seem to be more passive than active in their relations to one another; these relations are, after all, unchanging, always the same. Likewise, Aquinas never carried over his understanding of divine persons as subsistent relations to the world of human persons and other subjects of experience in this world. In his view, people and things first have to be themselves before they can relate to others in various ways. Relations to others, accordingly, may be somewhat important but they are not in any sense of the word constitutive of who or what one is here and now as in the case of the

---

[6] Daly, *Beyond God the Father*, 33.
[7] See Aquinas, *Summa Theologiae*, I, question 29, art. 4.

divine persons in their relations to one another. In still another way, therefore, Aquinas implicitly favored the thing- or noun-oriented approach to reality already found in the philosophy of Plato and Aristotle. The value of a verb-oriented approach to reality suggested by the image of three divine persons in dynamic relation to one another was thus lost from sight, not only for Aquinas but also for many of his followers even to the present day.

In one of her later books *Gyn/Ecology*, Daly has the following incisive comments on the use of the term "procession" to describe the relations between Father, Son, and Spirit within classical trinitarian theology:

> According to Christian theology, there are processions within the godhead, which is triune. The son, who is the second person, is said to proceed from the father, and the holy ghost is said to proceed from the father and the son. Moreover, all creatures proceed from this eternally processing god, who is their Last End, with whom the righteous will be united in eternal bliss. Thus, in this symbol system there is a circular pattern/model for muted existence: separation from and return to the same immutable source.[8]

Patriarchy, the "procession" of everything from the Father and the eventual return of all things to the Father as the final goal of life in this world, thus reigns supreme within the Christian worldview.

Yet even here so much depends upon whether one is thinking within a verb-oriented or a noun-oriented context. Within a verb-oriented context, for example, processions are positive. They are a sign of movement, a sharing of feeling and life, between the cause and the effect. Within a noun-oriented context, processions are negative; they point to fixed structures and hierarchical order between people and things. So in the end it comes down to how one understands the workings of causes and effects. Within the static noun-oriented approach to reality, causes and effects are inevitably separate from one another in time and sometimes also in space, with the cause always existing prior to the effect. The effect is then dependent upon the cause for its own subsequent existence. Within a more dynamic verb-oriented approach to reality, causes and effects are not separated in time and space but always linked together as ongoing interdependent realities. The effect has as much influence on

---

[8] Mary Daly, *Gyn/Ecology: The Metaethics of Radical Feminism* (Boston: MA: Beacon Press, 1990), 37.

the cause as the cause has on the effect. Neither is superior to the other since both codetermine what actually happens.[9] Within this verb-oriented context, accordingly, "procession" is not a negative word as Daly maintains, but something positive, pointing to movement and life for both cause and effect.

Two More Sources of Sexism in the Church

As for the other two issues raised by Daly in *Beyond God the Father*, she is certainly correct in her insistence that the Genesis account of the fall of Adam and Eve "has projected a malignant image of the male-female relationship and of the 'nature' of women that is still deeply embedded in the modern psyche."[10] Likewise, Daly rightly notes that women as a result suffer from a divided consciousness, feeling guilty when they have done nothing wrong; hence, they must consciously choose to think and act otherwise.[11] But isn't more needed to affirm with confidence that "female is beautiful"? Why not completely rethink the meaning of the Genesis story about eating fruit from the tree of knowledge of good and evil (Gen 2:17)? What is coming to knowledge of good and evil, after all, but the dawn of freedom and rational self-consciousness, the awareness of being able to make one's own choices, whether for good or for evil? Understood this way, the Genesis story tells us that Eve prior to Adam took the necessary first step toward human maturity, a step that de facto ended in pain and suffering but still held great promise for the future of the human race.[12]

With respect to Daly's charge that classical christology is really "Christolatry," a diversion from the true worship of God, there is once

---

[9] To his credit, Aquinas had this insight not only with respect to the relations of the divine persons to one another but with respect to all self-contained activities within the world of creation. For example, in the act of seeing the seer and the one seen are dynamically one, just as in the act of thinking the intellect and the thing thought are one (cf. *Summa Theologiae*, I, question 85, art. 2). But with respect to transient activity where the actor and the thing acted upon are separate realities, Aquinas followed Aristotle in giving ontological priority to the cause over the effect. The God-world relationship for Aquinas is thus governed by the Aristotelian understanding of external cause-effect relationships.

[10] Daly, *Beyond God the Father*, 45.

[11] Ibid., 47–51.

[12] See here Paul Tillich, *Systematic Theology*, vol. 2 (Chicago: University of Chicago Press, 1957), 29–44, where he conceives original sin as a symbolic representation of the transition from the state of "dreaming innocence" to finite self-actualization that always involves a sense of loss as well as growth in freedom and self-knowledge.

again much to ponder. "The idea of a unique male savior may be seen as one more legitimation of male superiority. Indeed, there is reason to see it as a perpetuation of patriarchal religion's 'original sin' of servitude to patriarchy itself."[13] Daly's solution to this problem is to reinterpret the classical Christian doctrine of the Second Coming. The end of the world will not be the Second Coming of Christ, but the Second Coming of the Great Mother, the repressed tradition of goddess worship within human religious consciousness.[14] Daly has in mind the response of the noted Swiss psychologist Karl Jung to the proclamation of the dogma of the Assumption of Mary into heaven by the Catholic Church: "Symbolically and socially, women have been identified with matter, sex, and evil. Jung saw the Assumption as saying No to these assumptions, challenging the false innocence of the God and godly whose identity depends upon non-identification with women."[15] But the deeper question is still whether, as Daly herself admits, simply calling God Mother rather than Father is the answer to the problem of sexism in the church. What does it mean to be fully human, whether as a woman or as a man?

Would it not be of some value first to ask what Jesus himself really stood for as the alleged archetypal symbol of God and how being male rather than female may have made a difference in getting across that message? Daly focuses upon the traditional understanding of Jesus as a sacrificial victim who died on the cross to redeem humankind from their sins and comments: "While the image of sacrificial victim may inspire saintliness in a few, in the many the effect seems to be to evoke intolerance. That is, rather than being enabled to imitate the sacrifice of Jesus, they feel guilt and transfer this to the 'Other,' thus making the latter 'imitate' Jesus in the role of scapegoat."[16] That is, men get rid of guilt feelings for doing something wrong by blaming the women in their lives for whatever happened. There is much here that rings true to human experience. But what about all those men and women who achieved some degree of sanctity (and thus self-transcendence) through imitating the self-sacrificing love of Jesus for his fellow human beings? Do they have something to tell the rest of us about the deeper meaning of human life? Nancey Murphy and George Ellis, one a professional theologian

[13] Daly, *Beyond God the Father*, 71.

[14] Ibid., 82–97.

[15] Ibid., 89. See also C. G. Jung, "A Psychological Approach to the Dogma of the Trinity," in *Psychology and Religion: West and East*, trans. R. F. C. Hull, 2nd ed. (Princeton, NJ: Princeton University Press, 1969), 164–200.

[16] Daly, *Beyond God the Father*, 76.

and the other a recognized scientist, claim that "[s]elf-renunciation for the sake of the other is humankind's highest good" and as a result is the unconscious driving force of cosmic evolution.[17] Murphy and Ellis thus endorse nonviolence as the only effective way to solve nasty conflict situations in human life. They know that this way of proceeding is countercultural, but they advocate it anyway because they believe that it is the core message of the Gospel: the triune God's total self-giving to humankind in the person of Jesus.[18]

But if nonviolence and the service of others is the right way for human beings to deal with one another, could a woman at the time of Jesus communicate that message as well as a man? In my judgment, probably not, but only because most men and at least some women would have misunderstood what she was trying to say. Women, after all, were supposed to find self-fulfillment in serving the men in their lives. But when Jesus as a male asserts: "For the Son of Man did not come to be served but to serve and to give his life as a ransom for many" (Mark 10:45), that is clearly countercultural, a shocking reversal of conventional goals and values for human life even to this day. Hence, the deeper reason for the incarnation of God as a male human being is not the innate superiority of men to women but, ironically, their customary inferiority to women in exhibiting through their day-to-day behavior the true image of God. Only a male like Jesus could paradoxically use his maleness to get across the deeper meaning of human life for both men and women.[19]

Rosemary Radford Ruether: God as the Divine Ground of Being

Turning now to other feminists with a background in Christian theology, I first cite the work of Rosemary Radford Ruether. She formulated what has come to be known as the "critical principle of feminist theology":

---

[17] See Nancey Murphy & George F. R. Ellis, *On the Moral Nature of the Universe: Theology, Cosmology, and Ethics* (Minneapolis, MN: Fortress, 1996), 118, 202–5.

[18] Ibid., 173–201.

[19] See here Sandra M. Schneiders, *Women and the Word* (New York: Paulist Press, 1986), 70: "Men are challenged by Jesus to reject the cultural definition of masculinity as well as all the patriarchal structures and behaviors which flow from it. Women are challenged to develop a renewed sense of themselves as adult children of God made in the divine image . . . The traits and virtues which women have experienced as marks of inferiority need to be seen in the light of the life-style of Jesus who validates them and proposes them to both men and women as the praxis of the reign of God."

> The critical principle of feminist theology is the promotion of the
> full humanity of women. Whatever denies, diminishes, or distorts
> the full humanity of women is, therefore, appraised as not redemp-
> tive . . . This negative principle also implies the positive principle:
> what does promote the full humanity of women is of the Holy, it
> does reflect relation to the divine, it is the true nature of things, the
> authentic message of redemption and the mission of redemptive
> community.[20]

This is a marvelously concise statement of purpose and direction for all
those who want to affirm the basic equality of women (and men) before
God rather than to argue about the intrinsic superiority of the one sex
over the other. But not everyone would agree with Ruether in her further
comments about the nature of God and the God-world relationship. For
she prefers to think of God in impersonal terms: "God is not a 'being'
removed from creation, ruling it from outside in the manner of a patriarchal ruler; God is the source of being that underlies creation and
grounds its nature and future potential for continual transformative
renewal."[21]

Likewise, in *Sexism and God-Talk* she professes agnosticism about the
possibility of personal immortality, subjective life after death: "our existence ceases as individuated ego/organism and dissolves back into the
cosmic matrix of matter/energy, from which the new centers of individu-
ation arise. It is this matrix, rather than our individuated centers of being,
that is 'everlasting,' that subsists underneath the coming to be and pass-
ing away of individual beings and even planetary worlds."[22] Yet she also
asks: "If the interiority of our organism is a personal center, how much
more so is the great organism of the universe itself? . . . That great collective personhood is the Holy Being in which our achievements and
failures are gathered up, assimilated into the fabric of being, and carried
forward into new possibilities."[23] In any case, Ruether is not in favor of
retaining the doctrine of the Trinity as part of the Christian heritage for
the future. God understood as the divine ground of being is our best

---

[20] Rosemary Radford Ruether, *Sexism and God-Talk: Toward a Feminist Theology*
(Boston, MA: Beacon Press, 1983), 18–19.

[21] Rosemary Radford Ruether, *Women and Redemption: A Theological History* (Minneapolis, MN: Fortress Press, 1998), 223.

[22] Ruether, *Sexism and God-Talk*, 257.

[23] Ibid., 258.

hope for achieving a new sense of humanity for both women and men and for averting an ecological crisis in the use of natural resources.[24]

Sallie McFague: God as the "Soul" of the World

Sallie McFague, on the contrary, seeks to convert the image of a distant patriarchal God prevalent within classical Christianity into the new image of a unipersonal God immanent within the world as its "soul" or animating principle.[25] She favors such a personal understanding of God because it is "the only metaphor we know from the inside; there is nothing that we can say about God with the help of any other model that has the same credibility to us, because there is no other aspect of the universe that we know in the same way, with the privilege of the insider."[26] At the same time, in line with the thinking of process theologians (see chap. 5) she believes that precisely as personal God "has intrinsic relations with all else that exists . . . God is present in and to the world as the kind of other, the kind of Thou, much closer to a mother, lover, or friend than to a king or lord."[27] In thus choosing three interrelated feminine images of God, McFague introduces something of a trinitarian dimension into her model of God, but this should not be unduly emphasized since in line with the notion of God as the "soul" of the universe they represent more three "faces" or appearances of God to her creatures than three distinct persons as within the classical doctrine of the Trinity.

The Doctrine of the Trinity as an Asset to Christian Feminists

Letty Russell and Patricia Wilson-Kastner, however, are much stronger in their affirmation of the classical doctrine of the Trinity as a valuable asset within Christian feminism. In *Human Liberation in a Feminist Perspective*, Russell makes reference to the three divine persons as Creator, Lib-

---

[24] Rosemary Radford Ruether, *New Woman/New Earth: Sexist Ideologies and Human Liberation* (New York: Seabury Press, 1975), 186–211. See also her book *Gaia and God: An Ecofeminist Theology of Earth Healing* (San Francisco: HarperCollins, 1992), 255, where she speaks of "two voices of divinity from nature": the masculine voice of God and the feminine voice of *Gaia*.

[25] Sallie McFague, *Models of God: Theology for an Ecological, Nuclear Age* (Philadelphia: Fortress Press, 1987), ix–xiv, 63–78.

[26] Ibid., 82.

[27] Ibid., 83–84.

erator, and Sanctifier within the "economic" Trinity (the Trinity as related to us) and claims that even within the "immanent" Trinity the divine persons in their internal relations to one another "can be said to transcend, and also to include, all the characteristics familiar to us by analogy to human love."[28] Thus all three divine persons transcend and yet exemplify what it means to be alternately masculine and feminine. Then in *The Future of Partnership* Russell notes: "The characteristics of partnership, or *koinonia*, may be discovered in their perfection in the Trinity, where there is a focus of relationship in mutual love between the persons and toward creation."[29] Thus women and men are encouraged to adopt a new sense of partnership with one another and with the divine persons in bringing about the New Creation.

Even more emphatically, Patricia Wilson-Kastner claims that "the Trinity is more supportive of feminist values than is a strict monotheism. Popular monotheism is by far more of a support for patriarchy than trinitarianism, because the one God is always imaged as male."[30] Imaging the divine persons as "three centers of awareness and centeredness who are also perfectly open and interdependent on each other"[31] encourages one to focus on "personal interrelationship as the foundation of God's interaction with the world."[32] Therefore, it is not the solitary ruler or Unmoved Mover of classical theology but the Trinity as family or community incorporating within itself a diverse and interrelated creation that becomes normative for the God-world relationship.

At the very end of her analysis of the doctrine of the Trinity from a feminist perspective, Wilson-Kastner discusses the key issue of the language to be used in referring to the divine persons:

> Language, as feminists are acutely aware, communicates affective dimensions as well as cognitive ones. Because of this phenomenon, inclusiveness in language about God does not mean that each word or phrase about the trinitarian God must be sex-neutral or have male and female (or exclusively female) terms side by side. Inclusiveness

[28] Letty M. Russell, *Human Liberation in a Feminist Perspective* (Philadelphia, PA: Westminster Press, 1974), 102.

[29] Letty M. Russell, *The Future of Partnership* (Philadelphia, PA: Westminster Press, 1979), 35.

[30] Patricia Wilson-Kastner, *Faith, Feminism, and the Christ* (Philadelphia, PA: Fortress Press, 1983), 122.

[31] Ibid., 126.

[32] Ibid., 124.

requires that old and new language be used in worship, teaching, and theological endeavors.[33]

Elizabeth Johnson: God as She Who Is

Perhaps the most successful feminist writer to use an alternate language for the divine persons in their relations with their (human) creatures is Elizabeth Johnson in her widely read book *She Who Is*.[34] The title, to be sure, might lead one to think that she thinks of God in strictly unipersonal terms. But such is not the case since a major part of the book is dedicated to an exposition of the three divine persons as Spirit-Sophia, Jesus-Sophia, and Mother-Sophia. *Sophia*, of course, is the Greek term for divine wisdom, which in the Hebrew Bible is personified as female (e.g., Wis 6–10). It stands in contrast to *Logos*, the Greek term for the Divine Word, either spoken or written, which is symbolically masculine. Hence, by referring to God as "She Who Is" rather than "He Who Is," and by using *Sophia* rather than *Logos* as the generic term for God, Johnson is setting up an alternative language to describe the reality of God.

Her point, however, is not to claim that God is female rather than male or even that there is a feminine dimension to God but only to legitimate use of female images to describe the transcendent reality of God who is neither male nor female:

> The mystery of God transcends all images but can be spoken about equally well or poorly in concepts taken from male or female reality. The approach advocated here proceeds with the insight that only if God is so named, only if the full reality of women as well as men enters into the symbolization of God along with symbols from the natural world, can the idolatrous fixation on one image be broken and the truth of the mystery of God, in tandem with the liberation of all human beings and the whole earth, emerge for our time.[35]

Irrespective of their specific names (whether male, female, or neuter), accordingly, the divine persons exist in ongoing communion with one another and as such offer to human beings the ideal of a perfect community in which all members share equally: "In the end, the Trinity

---

[33] Ibid., 134.

[34] Elizabeth A. Johnson, *She Who Is: The Mystery of God in Feminist Theological Discourse* (New York: Crossroad, 1992).

[35] Ibid., 56.

provides a symbolic picture of totally shared life at the heart of the universe . . . Mutual relationship of different equals appears as the ultimate paradigm of personal and social life. The Trinity as pure relationality, moreover, epitomizes the connectedness of all that exists in the universe.[36]

Conclusion

There is a tension, to be sure, in Johnson's thought between the affirmation of the unity of God (She Who Is) and the counter-affirmation of the plurality and diversity of the divine persons (Spirit-Sophia, Jesus-Sophia, Mother-Sophia). Johnson herself claims that God is Holy Mystery and as such the reality of God can never be captured in a single image or set of images.[37] But, as I have commented elsewhere,[38] within these limits a more explicit philosophy of intersubjectivity, such as that proposed in Colin Gunton's *The One, the Three and the Many* and in my own rethinking of the philosophy of Alfred North Whitehead (see chap. 6), might be very useful as a theoretical underpinning for Johnson's efforts to establish the doctrine of the Trinity as the centerpiece of her feminist theology. In any case, along with Letty Russell and Patricia Wilson-Kastner, Elizabeth Johnson has made abundantly clear that, properly understood, the doctrine of the Trinity is no obstacle but rather an unexpected aid to the human flourishing of women, their full humanity in this world.[39]

---

[36] Ibid., 222. See also 52–54 where Johnson critiques the otherwise well-intentioned efforts of Leonardo Boff (cf. *The Maternal Face of God: The Feminine and Its Religious Expressions*, trans. Robert Barr and John Diercksmeier [Maryknoll, NY: Orbis, 1987]) and Donald Gelpi (cf. *The Divine Mother: A Trinitarian Theology of the Holy Spirit* [Lanham, MD: University Press of America, 1984]) to introduce a feminine dimension into the Christian understanding of God since they unconsciously limit the potential of women to move beyond traditional stereotypes of womanhood and femininity in their personal lives.

[37] Ibid., 104–20.

[38] Bracken, "The Theology of God of Elizabeth A. Johnson," in *Things New and Old: Essays on the Theology of Elizabeth A. Johnson*, eds. Phyllis Zagano and Terrence W. Tilley (New York: Crossroad, 1999), 21–38.

[39] No mention was made in this chapter of the groundbreaking work of Elisabeth Schüssler Fiorenza in her much-acclaimed book *In Memory of Her: A Feminist Theological Reconstruction of Christian Origins*, 10th ed. (New York: Crossroad, 2000) and other writings, since her basic focus has not been on feminism and the doctrine of the Trinity but on covert references within the New Testament to the leadership role of women in the early church.

Chapter Eight

Perichoresis of the World Religions

Another contemporary challenge to the doctrine of the Trinity as the appropriate Christian understanding of God comes from Christians seeking common ground with proponents of the other world religions in the effort to work together for a better world. Given the paradoxical notion of three persons who are still only one God, why not, at least for the moment, "shelve" the doctrine of the Trinity so as to make common cause with Jews, Muslims, and other monotheists in order to address the more urgent issue of atheistic materialism and its consequences in our world? The problem, of course, is that also sitting at the interreligious dialogue table will be representatives of the East Asian religions (Hinduism, Buddhism, Confucianism, and Taoism) who seem to endorse either polytheism (belief in many gods) or some transpersonal reality (e.g., Brahman, Nirvana, the Tao). Keeping this in mind, Paul Knitter roughly twenty years ago proposed that *soteria* (Greek for "salvation") could serve as the common ground, or at least the best starting point, for interreligious dialogue. By *soteria* he means "promoting human welfare and bringing about liberation with and for the poor and nonpersons."[1]

In this way he simultaneously finds a focus for conversation of theists with nontheists about common human concerns and links interreligious

---

[1] Paul F. Knitter, "Toward a Liberationist Theology of Religion," in *The Myth of Christian Uniqueness*, ed. Paul Knitter and John Hick (Maryknoll, NY: Orbis Books, 1987), 187. By his own admission, this is an extension of his thought in an earlier book-length publication, *No Other Name: A Critical Survey of Christian Attitudes Toward the World Religions* (Maryknoll, NY: Orbis Books, 1985).

dialogue with liberation theology, the effort to mobilize the resources of Christian theology on behalf of the rights of the poor and oppressed peoples of this earth.

Evaluation and Critique of Paul Knitter's Approach

Remarkable as it was in terms of providing a new sense of direction and purpose for interreligious dialogue, Knitter's proposal was still not fully accepted by others in the field. James Fredericks, for example, notes:

> By placing his money on the "well being of the poor and non-persons" as the central value for evaluating religions, Knitter is suggesting that the real differences that distinguish religious believers are not theoretical or doctrinal but ethical. Furthermore, Buddhists and Muslims, Christians and Confucians who are committed to justice may well have more in common with one another than they do with their own coreligionists who do not have such commitments.[2]

There are, accordingly, problems lying just beneath the surface in this well-meant linkage of interreligious dialogue (which presupposes deep respect for the sincere religious beliefs of other people) and liberation theology (with its outspoken agenda of securing economic and political justice for the poor and oppressed of this world). Is it right, for example, for a socially conscious Christian to criticize a Hindu who supports the caste system in India on the basis of select texts in the Vedas, the sacred Hindu scriptures?[3] Yet if in the interests of interreligious dialogue one acquiesces in a social system that in one's judgment discriminates against large numbers of people in the Indian subcontinent, is one merely paying lip service to the demands of liberation theology?

Fredericks's own approach is to turn away from classical theology of religion as practiced by exclusivists (those who believe that salvation is to be found only in formal adherence to Jesus as one's Lord and Savior),

---

[2] James L. Fredericks, *Faith among Faiths: Christian Theology and Non-Christian Religions* (New York: Paulist Press, 1999), 70.

[3] See, e.g., the famous Purusha-sukta in the Rig Veda in which the gods create the world by dismembering the primeval Man: "His mouth became the Brahmin; his arms were made into the Warrior, his thighs the People, and from his feet the Servants were born," in *Sacred Texts of the World: A Universal Anthology*, eds. Ninian Smart and Richard D. Hecht (New York: Crossroad, 1997), 213.

inclusivists (those who claim that salvation is available in non-Christian religions but only because God who is most fully revealed in the person of Jesus is likewise implicitly at work in these other traditions), and pluralists (those who believe that all the world religions are legitimate vehicles for human self-transcendence toward Ultimate Reality). Instead, says Fredericks, one should practice comparative theology, that is, "the attempt to understand the meaning of Christian faith by exploring it in the light of other religious traditions."[4] It is too soon in the history of interreligious dialogue to pass judgment on the beliefs of others or, after the manner of pluralists, to assert what is (or at least should be) the deeper meaning of Ultimate Reality that is implicitly sought by all the religious traditions in different ways. Rather, one should simply be content not only to learn about other religions but also to learn from the beliefs and practices of these other religions by way of enriching one's own religious experience: "By comparing their own faith with the faith of other religious believers, Christians can deepen their own religious lives and come to a better understanding of the Gospel. And in the very process of doing this, Christians will come to a deeper knowledge and appreciation of believers who follow other religious paths."[5] Only thus will Christians develop the practical skills needed to live responsibly and creatively with their non-Christian friends and neighbors and thereby help to create the better world advocated by Knitter and other liberation theologians.

Fredericks's approach to interreligious dialogue has much to recommend it and has been effectively endorsed by other scholars in the field.[6] Likewise, Knitter himself has words of commendation for the merit of this "acceptance" approach to interreligious dialogue, even as he continues to espouse his own "mutuality" or basically pluralist position.[7] Perhaps a combination of the two approaches is what is needed here and now. Ethical concerns such as the alleviation of poverty and political oppression around the world, as Knitter suggests, cannot be postponed until all doctrinal disagreements among representatives of the world religions are settled. Yet, as Frederick urges, the best way to learn both

---

[4] Fredericks, *Faith among Faiths*, 139.

[5] Ibid., 167.

[6] See, e.g., Francis X. Clooney, SJ, *Theology After Vedanta: An Experiment in Comparative Theology* (Albany: State University of New York Press, 1993), 4–9; likewise, in a somewhat more popular vein by the same author, *Hindu Wisdom for All God's Children* (Maryknoll, NY: Orbis Books, 1998).

[7] See, e.g., Paul F. Knitter, *Introducing Theologies of Religion* (Maryknoll, NY: Orbis Books, 2002), 173–237.

about and from religious traditions other than one's own is to risk conversation with the members of other religious traditions precisely on points of disagreement as well as matters of common concern.[8] In any event, in keeping with the theme of this book, I will now summarize and critique what might be called a trinitarian solution to the issue of "salvation" within the various world religions. Then, still working from within a trinitarian perspective, I will offer some modest changes that might address the objections of some non-Christians that a trinitarian approach to interreligious dialogue is still one more example of Christian "imperialism" toward the other world religions.

S. Mark Heim: Multiple Ways to be Saved

S. Mark Heim, like Fredericks, is suspicious of the claim that Christians engaged in interreligious dialogue can be neatly classified as either exclusivists, inclusivists, or pluralists (cf. above, pp. 95–96). Perhaps they all make the same mistake in thinking that salvation has to be the same for everyone irrespective of their religious beliefs.[9] Hence, they argue interminably about whether in the end there is only one way to salvation or whether there are many roughly equal ways to salvation. But they never ask themselves whether salvation for a Muslim or Jew, or even more dramatically, for a Hindu or Buddhist, is the same as salvation for a Christian. If a Jew or Muslim, for example, goes to "heaven," will they join Christians in worshiping Jesus as their Lord and Savior? If a Buddhist attains Nirvana, is that the same as enjoying communion with a personal God?

Heim's proposal is that "salvation" means different things in different religions and that these different religious "ends" are all valid and real.[10] At the same time, he claims that Jesus Christ is the Savior of the world. He is not thereby involved in a contradiction, because in his view the ends or goals of the other world religions correspond to different dimensions of the divine life of the triune God: "They become separate ends by virtue of isolation and limitation, but this does not compromise their reality. Because the nature of God is a communion of the three divine persons,

---

[8] See, however, Knitter, *Introducing Theologies of Religion*, 224–37, where he raises critical questions about the adequacy of the "acceptance" model for interreligious dialogue.

[9] S. Mark Heim, *The Depth of the Riches: A Trinitarian Theology of Religious Ends* (Grand Rapids, MI: Eerdmans, 2001), 3–6.

[10] Ibid., 7.

that nature itself has a variety of dimensions."[11] This is an intriguing proposal because it allows a Christian to give full respect and even reverence for the beliefs of the members of other world religions and at the same time to claim that they are in fact unknowingly addressing the same God as the Christian, albeit under a different dimension or perspective. Heim reserves the term "salvation" to Christian belief in the triune God, but its equivalent in terms of "religious aim" or "religious fulfillment" is in his view offered by the triune God to the adherents of the other world religions.[12]

Let us summarize his basic argument. Heim begins by noting that for Christians salvation is "communion with God and God's creatures through Christ Jesus."[13] But he likewise claims that for non-Christians such a claim does not have much appeal. Rather, some other religious end appeals to them and is the source of their quest for self-fulfillment. They would thus be very disappointed if at the moment of death they had to admit that they were seriously mistaken in their pursuit of religious self-fulfillment and that they now must follow the lead of Christians in professing Jesus as their Lord and Savior. Why then should the divine persons not allow sincere non-Christians to find their religious fulfillment in something other than full interpersonal communion with themselves through the person of Jesus? Provided that the spiritual quest of non-Christians leads them to contact with the reality of the triune God one way or another, why not respect the freedom of non-Christians to find ultimate self-fulfillment in line with their own lifelong religious beliefs?[14]

But will they be aware of the choices of other human beings, notably of Christians, who seem to have made a better choice, and will they as a result be envious and thus not be very happy in heaven after all? Heim's argument here is intriguing. He first appeals to the way in which Dante in *The Divine Comedy* depicts people in heaven and hell as a matter of personal choice on their part:

> In the *Comedy*, everything happens by attraction, by free affinity and desire. No one is sent to hell or bound there by external force, just as no one is bored or uneasy in heaven . . . Sounds of anguish echo from some circles of hell. But whenever Dante stops to talk with its inhabitants, he finds that God is not afflicting them. Rather it is the

[11] Ibid., 9.
[12] Ibid., 8.
[13] Ibid., 19.
[14] Ibid., 76–77.

sin, to which they resolutely cling, that torments. There is bitter complaint, but not the slightest interest in change.[15]

People in hell cannot hurt others as they may have done while on earth, but they are certainly free to continue hurting themselves by their stubborn refusal to change their minds. By way of contrast,

> the relation with God that characterizes heaven is one that is unhesitatingly open to others' relation with God and to the various dimensions of God's relation with creation . . . It is each one's relation with God that makes possible and sustains this intercommunion among them, through which in turn their individual experiences and capacities are multiplied to allow the fullest communion with God.[16]

Applying this line of thought to analysis of the world religions, Heim speculates that Muslims and Jews in heaven will appreciate what Christians are experiencing through interpersonal communion with the divine persons, but they will still choose to relate to God as a single divine Agent rather than as a community of persons because of their history of relationship to God as unipersonal during their time on earth.[17] In similar fashion, Hindus, Buddhists, and Taoists who pursued loss of the self and absorption into Ultimate Reality in their lifetimes will understand in heaven what Christians, Jews, and Muslims worship in terms of God as personal, but they will still feel drawn to the Godhead, the mystical dimension of the divine being beyond personhood.[18] Finally, Christians in heaven will be able to appreciate what Hindus, Buddhists, and Taoists find attractive in the "emptiness" of the Godhead, and to what Jews and Muslims are drawn in worshiping God as the transcendent One. But at the same time Christians will find their own natural satisfaction in sharing the interpersonal life of the three divine persons.[19]

Different Dimensions of One and the Same Divine Life

Heim relies heavily here on the work of Ninian Smart and Steven Konstantine's *Christian Systematic Theology in a World Context*. Smart and

---

[15] Ibid., 101.
[16] Ibid., 108.
[17] Ibid., 192–95.
[18] Ibid., 186–89.
[19] Ibid., 195–97.

Konstantine argue that there are three different dimensions of the divine life: "The first dimension is what they [Smart and Konstantine] call the infinity of the divine life as it circulates through the three persons . . . The second aspect of the divine life they describe is the plurality of the three persons themselves, and their relations with each other . . . The third is the common will or the collective 'I' of the Trinity according to which God acts with perfect unity of purpose."[20] All three dimensions are an integral part of the full divine life. But human beings will inevitably focus on one of these dimensions rather than the other two in their relation to God (or, more generically, to Ultimate Reality). Within some forms of Hinduism, Buddhism, and Taoism, for example, the focus will be on the infinity of the divine life, the impersonal dimension of the triune God. Within Christianity, the focus will normally be on the relations of Father, Son, and Holy Spirit to one another. Finally, within Judaism and Islam the focus will be on the common will or collective "I" of the divine persons in dealing with creation. All these religions are de facto centered on some dimension of the triune God, but only Christians are aware that what they are worshiping is indeed one God in three persons.

Will Christians Have a Higher Place in Heaven?

Does this mean that Christians, so to speak, will have "a higher place in heaven" than the members of other world religions? Heim's comments are worth pondering. On the one hand, there is no hierarchical order among the dimensions of the divine life: "It is possible to have a firm hold on the personal dimension of the divine life and to be wanting in an adequate grasp of its impersonal dimension."[21] A Buddhist, for example, may have a much deeper experience of the impersonal reality of God (without, of course, thinking of it as an experience of God rather than as an experience of Nirvana) than a Christian, Jew, or Muslim will have of God as personal. So there is no intrinsic reason for the members of one religion to claim superiority over the members of other religions on the grounds of a higher insight into the nature of Ultimate Reality. All the world religions have valid insights into Transcendent Reality. But, on the other hand, since the notion of "communion" is so important for understanding the reality of God as triune, and since "communion"

[20] Ibid., 157. See also Ninian Smart and Steven Konstantine, *Systematic Theology in a World Context* (Minneapolis, MN: Fortress Press, 1991), 167–74.

[21] Heim, *The Depth of the Riches*, 213.

always implies a unity-in-diversity of parts or members wherever it is found, then Christians might be better positioned to accept the beliefs about God or Ultimate Reality coming from the members of other world religions than these individuals in turn would be accepting of the Christian belief that God is triune.[22]

Buddhists or Hindus, for example, might be convinced that concrete images of the Buddha or of Hindu gods and goddesses are merely instrumental to the attainment of a deeper insight into the ultimate transpersonal reality of the Buddha nature or of *Brahman*. But, at least in principle, a Christian should acknowledge the impersonal as well as the personal reality of God, the reality of the Godhead or the divine nature as well as the reality of the three divine persons. Similarly, a Christian can profess belief in God as One along with Jews and Muslims, but they in turn will presumably find it more difficult to accept the reality of God as three persons in community.[23] So insofar as Christians are (or at least can be) more inclusive in their acceptance of the validity of other religious traditions, they may enjoy a "higher place in heaven," provided that they accept the challenge implicit in believing that God is indeed a perfect "communion" of three quite different divine persons, hence, a model of unity-in-diversity.[24]

Will Everyone Be Saved?

But does this mean that in the end everyone will be "saved," that everyone will somehow enjoy eternal life, no matter what their personal religious beliefs or lack thereof? Heim says no, indicating that there are four quite different "destinies" or "final ends" for human beings at the close of their lives on earth. There are those who find communion with God and all creation through Christ and thus achieve salvation in the proper sense. There are others who pursue "alternative religious ends" in line with their specific non-Christian religious beliefs and thus are "saved" for eternal union with God in a qualified sense. There are still others who even in eternal life continue to cling to some illusory form of created reality (e.g., love of money, sexual pleasure, worldly success) and thus find themselves in "hells of idolatry" by their own free choice. Finally, there are those who totally reject their status as creatures of God

[22] Ibid., 213–14.
[23] Ibid., 216–19, 223–38.
[24] Ibid., 253–56.

and thus must be annihilated by God at the end of their lives on earth since there is no place for them within the kingdom of God.[25]

Here in Heim's vision of "the last things," of course, the faithful within other world religions may well find reason to complain that they are thereby made second-class citizens within eternal life. Unless they somehow convert to Christianity (either in this life or in eternity), they lose out on the fullness of what the three divine persons have in mind for their rational creatures. Heim is careful to say that those "whose home religious tradition is not Christianity naturally are nurtured in such a way as to focus on the distinctive aspect their faith emphasizes."[26] Hence, they will certainly be happy within eternal life, enjoying to the full that dimension of the triune God on which they focused while on earth. But the very fact that they are thus linked with the triune God under one dimension should open them up to the possibility of embracing the full reality of the triune God at some point: "Since each dimension of relation with God is rooted in the trinitarian nature, any particular connection with the triune life can flow increasingly and ultimately into that communion with all the dimensions of the triune God which constitute salvation."[27] Salvation in the full sense is thus a real possibility, even if not a necessity, for all religiously oriented human beings, given God's loving care for all human beings. But does this claim subtly subordinate non-Christians to Christians in the final analysis?

Still Another Trinitarian Approach to Interreligious Dialogue

At the beginning of this chapter, I suggested that there might be still another "trinitarian" interpretation of the relations of the different world religions to one another that might not be seen as imperialistic by non-Christians. Likewise, it has less to do with speculation about life after death (which can never be verified empirically) than with life here and now, the current relations of Christians with their non-Christian friends and neighbors. It might, of course, still be offensive to some non-Christians if only because it presupposes a trinitarian structure to reality and thereby an implicit belief in the objective reality of the Trinity. But from the Christian perspective of this book, it at least allows one not only

---

[25] Ibid., 272–73.
[26] Ibid., 268.
[27] Ibid.

to affirm the legitimacy of the various non-Christian world religions but likewise to understand why there are so many different world religions. It may not be simply a matter of divine respect for human free choice (as Heim suggests) but part of a bigger plan on the part of the divine persons to illuminate the mystery of the God-world relationship.

To make this clear, however, I will have to make use of a metaphysical approach to the God-world relationship, a move that Heim for his own reasons explicitly rejects:

> [T]he hypothesis of multiple religious ends is not committed to any particular metaphysical view. Obviously, the universe does have some ultimate character or order. One or more of the religions may in fact offer descriptions of that order that are substantially better than others. But the hypothesis requires only that the nature of reality be such as to allow humans to phenomenally realize varied religious ends.[28]

Yet metaphysical questions keep popping up within Heim's own theory. He proposes, for example, that the triune God "withdraws" from the world in the act of creation so as to allow human beings and other creatures the freedom to make their own decisions in independence of God.[29] But if God is infinite and thus without boundaries in space and time, how can God "withdraw" from the world? Likewise, how can God be simultaneously beyond personhood, a single divine Agent, and a community of persons, all at the same time?

At intervals in the preceding chapters I have proposed as a model for the God-world relationship the notion of panentheism, everything existing in God but distinct from God at the same time. Such an understanding of the God-world relationship, which is basically derived from the philosophy of Alfred North Whitehead but modified to accommodate a trinitarian understanding of the God-world relationship, might well be what we are looking for here. For if the three divine persons by their dynamic interrelation cocreate a divine field of activity or common "space" among themselves, and if creation comes into being within that space, then creatures can truly exist in God and yet be free to make their own decisions within their own finite space, even as they receive promptings (the equivalent of actual grace) from the divine persons on what

[28] Ibid., 24.
[29] Ibid., 247.

decisions here and now to make. Likewise, the three divine persons can be simultaneously interpersonal in their relations to one another, a single divine Agent in their joint activity toward their creatures, and yet have a transcendent dimension over and above personhood through sharing a common life that is at the same time the ground of being or vital source for the ever-changing world of creation within their midst. I will provide additional details for this scheme in the next chapter, but for now it is important only to see how this model of the God-world relationship can unexpectedly facilitate better dialogue among representatives of the various world religions.

Conclusion

Within this metaphysical scheme Ultimate Reality is not simply God but the simultaneous reality of God, the world of nature, and the world of human beings in *perichoresis*, dynamic interrelation (see chap. 2). Reality is thus equivalently "cosmotheandric," to use a term coined by Raimon Panikkar, one of the major scholars in contemporary interreligious dialogue:

> We are not God; God alone is God. But Christ is God's Son, one with the Father inasmuch as the divine mystery is pure gift, donation. . . . The whole universe is engaged in the process. In Christian language, the whole of reality is Father, Christ, and Holy Spirit. It is not only all the divine mysteries but likewise the whole mystery of creation that is held within the Christ—in a process of growth and maturation.[30]

This is not to deny the freedom of the divine persons to create or not to create, but only to affirm that, given the divine decision to create, God, the world of nature, and the world of human beings are intimately interconnected and interdependent.

Furthermore, all the world religions in their own way seem to acknowledge and affirm this "cosmotheandric" reality, this basically trinitarian structure of reality. Some religions, to be sure, focus more on the this-worldly character of this Ultimate Reality. Others like Judaism, Christianity, and Islam affirm more its other-worldly or transcendent

---

[30] Raimon Panikkar, *Christophany: The Fullness of Man* (Maryknoll, NY: Orbis Books, 2004), 139.

character. But all the world religions seem to be necessary so as to expand upon and illuminate the multidimensional character of Ultimate Reality.[31] Moreover, if all the world religions are thus needed to express the "cosmotheandric" character of this world, then a Christian can say in good conscience that it must be part of Divine Providence that there are many world religions, each with its own role to play within salvation history. As Panikkar comments, "Jesus is Christ, but Christ cannot be identified completely with Jesus of Nazareth."[32] Jesus is God's most perfect self-revelation to the world. But as a finite human being Jesus cannot fully embody the infinite reality of God. Christ as the full self-communication of God to the world must somehow also be found within the other world religions. The cosmotheandric reality composed of God, the world of nature, and the world of human beings in dynamic interrelation is thus revealed in the Christian doctrine of the Trinity. But that doctrine itself is still an imperfect human understanding and expression of the transcendent mystery of the God-world relationship in all its fullness.[33] Only in eternity will Christians and all other human beings finally understand in its fullness what they have consciously or unconsciously worshiped as Ultimate Reality in their own religious traditions.

[31] See here my article "Divine Providence and Human Freedom: A Second Look," *Theoforum* 35 (2004), 301–16, esp. 315–16. Likewise, see Jacques Dupuis, SJ, *Toward a Christian Theology of Religious Pluralism* (Maryknoll, NY: Orbis Books, 1997), 254–79.

[32] Panikkar, *Christophany*, 150. NB: This is, of course, not a full endorsement on my part of Panikkar's own approach to the doctrine of the Trinity as developed in earlier books. Cf., e.g., Raimundo Panikkar, *The Unknown Christ of Hinduism*, 2nd ed. (Maryknoll, NY: Orbis Books, 1981), 148–62, where Panikkar equates God the Father with Brahman and Christ with Isvara, the personalized reality of Brahman as object of worship for human beings. Hence, Panikkar seems to question whether there are three "persons" in the strict sense within God.

[33] See Dupuis, *Toward a Christian Theology of Religious Pluralism*, 259, 263. One can always object, of course, that envisioning Ultimate Reality as the combined reality of God, humanity, and the world of nature makes God finite since God is then only one factor in what constitutes Ultimate Reality. But as I see it, the present "cosmotheandric" reality only came about as the result of a free decision of the three divine persons to bring it into being and that there could have been already or could still be in the future other God-world relationships involving other universes and other rational species but always the same God. Infinity, in other words, has to do with the potentiality of subjects of experience to become other than what they are now rather than with the fixed actuality of an object of thought. Cf. on this point my earlier book *The Divine Matrix: Creativity as Link between East and West* (Maryknoll, NY: Orbis, 1995), 25–37, esp. n. 8 (p. 145), for an analysis and critique of the notion of infinity in the philosophy/theology of Thomas Aquinas.

Part Three

Trinitarian Theology for Today

Chapter Nine

Overcoming the Clash of Two Cultures

When Augustine interacted with the neo-Platonism of his day, he did not hesitate to modify its ideas, particularly in the light of his Christian belief in the Word made *flesh*. When Thomas Aquinas made use of the newly recovered insights of Aristotle in framing his doctrinal *Summa*, he felt free to not accept that philosopher's belief in the eternity of the world. It seems to me that those active today in the continuing dialogue between science and theology exhibit a similar openness to new knowledge and ways of thought while refusing to collude with the metascientific assumptions of an imperialist secularism that seeks to assert science as the only source of worthwhile knowledge.[1]

The Long-standing Connection between Religion and Science

John Polkinghorne, both physicist and Anglican priest, offered the above comments in an article for the fortieth anniversary celebration of the founding of ZYGON, one of the better-known journals for religion and science in the United States. As Polkinghorne sees it, theology and natural science have had considerable influence on one another over the centuries. The Christian doctrine of creation, for example, has been significantly altered by discoveries in cosmology and evolutionary biology.

[1] John Polkinghorne, "The Continuing Interaction of Science and Religion," ZYGON 40 (2005): 44.

At the same time, as we too have seen in chapter 3 of this book, the scientific revolution within Europe in the early modern era was carried on largely by scientists with antecedent religious beliefs in a Creator God and an orderly, law-abiding universe. Yet, as we also saw in the same chapter, later generations of natural scientists tended to separate religion and natural science to the point where neither side seemed to speak the same language anymore. This clash of cultures, in Polkinghorne's view, can be overcome provided that both sides acknowledge that they have something to learn from the other.

Scientists, for example, are beginning to realize that nature cannot be exhaustively explained through methodological reductionism, the analysis of wholes (entities of one kind or another) simply in terms of the interaction of component parts.[2] The whole in most cases is more than the sum of the parts. Above all, at higher levels of existence and activity within nature, where more complex physical organisms are in evidence, top-down causality seems to be just as important as bottom-up causality. That is, the entity as a whole seems to have an organizing principle or "soul" that directs the interrelated activity of the component parts. Yet the component parts still exercise bottom-up causality in limiting what can be done from the top down. My physical condition, for example, limits what I as a human being can think, say, and do here and now. It makes all the difference in the world whether I feel rested and calm or whether I am tired and upset when I am trying to make an important decision.

At the same time that scientists are uncovering the close connection between mind and body within human beings and other higher-order animal species, philosophers and theologians are beginning to move toward a new relational ontology or worldview in which things exist and flourish only in mutual interdependence.[3] For example, as already noted in chapter 4, there has been a new wave of interest among theologians in the doctrine of the Trinity, above all, in terms of the "social" model with its emphasis on relationality among the three divine persons. But if God is to be understood as a divine community, then the world of

---

[2] Ibid., 47.

[3] Ibid. See also Arthur Peacocke, *All That Is: A Naturalistic Faith for the Twenty-First Century*, ed. Philip Clayton (Minneapolis, MN: Fortress, 2007). This last book of a distinguished scientist/theologian, together with the commentaries on his work that were assembled by Clayton, gives a broad overview of the major issues in the contemporary religion and science debate.

creation as the collective image of God should likewise be understood in terms of interlocking communities and environments with individual entities as their component parts or members. The community, of course, cannot exist apart from the ongoing interplay of its component parts, but they in turn cannot long survive except as members of the larger social reality.

The Key Issue: The Relation between Matter and Spirit

So the stage seems to be set for fruitful dialogue between the proponents of religion and science, given this new awareness of relationality and interconnection within the world on both sides. But serious ground work needs to be done first. One of the controversial issues between natural scientists and philosopher/theologians, for example, is the relation between matter and spirit. Natural scientists tend to distrust the notion of spirit as something introduced by God or by some other supernatural agency as an organizing principle for material components. If it exists at all, spirit should be somehow emergent out of the interplay of the material components, not introduced from the outside as an immaterial principle.[4] But philosophers and theologians point out that if scientists do not admit the invisible workings of spirit in this world, then nature is nothing more than a "cosmic machine." Everything is programmed in terms of mathematically fixed laws and principles. If anything happens by chance, it is either ignored or integrated into some broader, strictly deterministic scheme. Thus free choice, and with it moral responsibility for human decisions, would seem to be merely an illusion.

A relational worldview that sees matter and spirit as somehow interconnected and mutually interdependent both in the world of nature and in human affairs is, accordingly, quite important for sustaining the right kind of dialogue between proponents of science and religion. Here I call attention to a point made in earlier chapters, namely, the notion of panentheism as a model for the God-world relationship. If creation exists within the triune God even as it maintains its distinction from the divine persons, then matter and spirit have to be somehow conjoined, exist in dynamic interrelation. God is evidently not a material entity within this world, and yet creation as a material reality exists within God, somehow

---

[4] See here Philip Clayton, *Mind and Emergence: From Quantum to Consciousness* (New York: Oxford University Press, 2004), for a historical survey and analysis of the notion of emergence of mind/spirit in the last century.

shares the divine life. So if God and creation coexist as a single complex reality (as suggested at the end of the last chapter), then there must be a deeper compatibility between matter and spirit that remains to be uncovered. The overriding question, of course, is how this is even conceivable. In what follows, I will explore further the neo-Whiteheadian understanding of panentheism that I have presented in earlier chapters and indicate how it could well be of real value for both natural scientists and Christian philosopher/theologians in their dialogue with one another.

Whitehead's Novel Approach to the Problem

Whitehead was a well-known mathematician and theoretical physicist before turning to the study of philosophy in his senior years. Hence, he was in an excellent position to evaluate what he called "the century of genius" within early modern Western science.[5] In the seventeenth century, roughly from Galileo to Newton, a new worldview emerged, dominated by mathematics and the quantitative analysis of the laws of nature.[6] But, said Whitehead, it was based on philosophical presuppositions that are open to question today. One of these premises is what he called "the fallacy of simple location," namely, that the world is made up of mini-things, inert bits of matter, which are simply located at individual points of space and time. These "atoms" have purely external relations to one another since they are separated from one another by space and time. Such purely external relations, of course, can be mathematically calculated in terms of "mass" and "force," thus giving rise to Newton's laws of motion in his *Principia naturalis philosophiae mathematica*. Furthermore, given such obvious success in measuring the forces of nature, many natural scientists even to this day do not further question to what extent the world of nature is in fact anything more than a "cosmic machine."[7]

---

[5] Alfred North Whitehead, *Science and the Modern World* (New York: Free Press, 1967), 39–55.

[6] Ibid., 48–50.

[7] See, however, Margaret J. Osler, "Mechanical Philosophy," in *Science and Religion: A Historical Introduction*, ed. Gary B. Ferngren (Baltimore, MD: John Hopkins University Press, 2002), 150. Osler points out that the notion of "force" as resident in bodies by reason of their "mass" was itself a departure from the strict principles of mechanical philosophy as inherited from Democritus and other ancient Greek philosophers.

Whitehead sought to counter this "fallacy" by proposing that the ultimate units of reality are not atoms or mini-things, parts of a gigantic machine, but instead "actual occasions," immaterial self-constituting subjects of experience that last only an instant but in that brief interval first grasp on a feeling level ("prehend") one another's presence and activity and then link up with one another to produce all the visible persons and things of this world for that moment.[8] In this way, for Whitehead the world is constituted not by things in combination but by inter-related events. Yet Whitehead himself may have fallen into still another fallacy in thus critiquing the thinking of his predecessors. For, if early modern scientists were guilty of implicitly endorsing philosophical materialism in identifying all of physical reality with tiny bits of matter being pushed and pulled in different directions, Whitehead may have ended up with an overly idealistic approach to reality, given his belief that "the final real things of which the world is made up"[9] are immaterial subjects of experience. In combination, they supposedly produce the material things of this world. But each such momentary subject of experience is still in a certain sense a world unto itself, somewhat akin to what G. W. Leibniz proposed with his controversial theory of "monads" in the eighteenth century.[10]

Thus, as Philip Clayton points out, Whitehead seems to be an idealist who excludes matter from his scheme almost as completely as early modern natural scientists excluded spirit from their analysis of the physical world.[11] What corresponds to the persons and things of common sense experience for Whitehead are simply aggregates of these immaterial subjects of experience with a "common element of form," a closely analogous pattern of existence and activity.[12] But if "societies" of such momentary subjects of experience have no external reality, something that endures over time and can be perceived by the senses, then physical reality as we understand it is an illusion. In the end, there are no material

---

[8] Whitehead, *Science and the Modern World*, 71–72. See also Whitehead, *Process and Reality*, 18.

[9] Whitehead, *Process and Reality*, 18.

[10] Whitehead, *Science and the Modern World*, 69. See also G. W. Leibniz, *The Monadology and Other Philosophical Writings*, trans. Robert Latta (London: Oxford University Press, 1951).

[11] Philip Clayton, "Eschatology as Metaphysics under the Guise of Hope," in *World Without End: Christian Eschatology from a Process Perspective*, ed. Joseph A. Bracken, SJ (Grand Rapids, MI: Eerdmans, 2005), 139–41.

[12] Whitehead, *Process and Reality*, 34.

substances, no things, but only groupings of immaterial subjects of experience. Whitehead, to be sure, claims that in his philosophy "it is not 'substance' which is permanent, but 'form.'"[13] But "form" seems likewise quite intangible unless it is embodied in something physical that lasts over time and can be sensibly felt.

Revision of Whitehead's Scheme

For this reason, I have argued for many years that Whiteheadian "societies" should be understood as energy fields that are objectively structured by the ongoing interplay of these momentary subjects of experience. Energy, after all, is a physical reality and when configured in specific ways it takes on the shape and form of the persons and things of ordinary experience. As Albert Einstein noted years ago, energy and mass are interchangeable. So to the extent that persons and things have mass or resistance to change, they are focal points for the conservation and transmission of energy. Furthermore, linked together in different ways, persons and things generate a vast array of interconnected energy fields. Admittedly, scientists do not always agree on the notion of a field. Some think, for example, that a field is simply a mental construct useful for assembling experimental data. Others claim that a field is always something physical and thus independent of the mind of the observer. As I use the term, "field" is indeed a physical reality that is both like and unlike what has been called in the past "substance." For, like the classical philosophical notion of substance, a field is by definition something that endures over space and time; yet unlike the classical notion of substance, it can likewise undergo over time a change in its basic structure or form as a result of the ongoing interaction of its component parts.

In any event, given this generic notion of field, I define the proper relation between spirit and matter as follows. By spirit I mean something that comes to be and continues to exist among multiple subjects of experience in dynamic interrelation. By matter I mean the structured field of activity set up by reason of their ongoing interaction. Matter is thus the objective self-expression of spirit when spirit is, as noted above, a social or intersubjective reality. Spirit arising out of intersubjective exchange is then the interior reality of matter. Spirit cannot exist apart from matter; matter cannot exist apart from spirit. They are in effect two sides of the same coin, two interrelated dimensions of one and the same corporate

---

[13] Ibid., 29.

reality. Even the reality of the triune God according to this theory has a "material" component, namely, the divine energy field set up and sustained by the ongoing relations of the three divine persons to one another from all eternity. Furthermore, as noted in earlier chapters, this divine energy field is at the same time the ground of being or vital source for the world of creation gradually taking shape within it. Matter emerges out of spirit and over time becomes more and more spiritualized without ever losing its base in material reality. We human beings with our highly sophisticated forms of communication with one another are, as Pierre Teilhard de Chardin proposed years ago in *The Phenomenon of Man*, gradually building up a sphere of mind (noosphere) on top of the biosphere in our world.[14]

Why This Makes a Difference

Here the reader may well respond: "Perhaps you are right, but what difference does it make for the sometimes stormy relations between proponents of religion and science? What is the cash value of such a proposal?" As I see it, its cash value is that it offers a comprehensive worldview within which both natural scientists and philosopher/theologians can be "at home" and mutually understand one another's arguments even if they do not always agree on the specific conclusions arising out of the argument in question. Scientists then cannot simply deny the reality of spirit at work in material things, and philosopher/theologians have to admit the strong influence of material reality on the workings of the spirit. But let us be more specific here.

A Philosophical Explanation for Emergent Monism?

Within the natural sciences at present, as already noted, one of the major issues is how to explain what has been called "emergent monism," the gradual growth in size and complexity of configurations of matter over the course of evolutionary history on this planet.[15] According to proponents of the standard big bang theory, for example, roughly three minutes after the initial explosion the nuclei of hydrogen and helium

---

[14] See Pierre Teilhard de Chardin, *The Phenomenon of Man*, trans. Bernard Wall, 2nd ed. (New York: Harper Torchbook, 1965), 237–90. A new edition and translation appeared in 1999: Pierre Teilhard de Chardin, *The Human Phenomenon*, trans. Sarah Appleton-Weber (Portland, OR: Sussex Academic Press).

[15] Cf., e.g., Clayton, *Mind and Emergence*, 38–64. See also Peacocke, *All That Is*, 12–16.

began to form out of the whirling mass of subatomic particles generated by the cooling down of the energy thus released.[16] After one billion years galaxies began to form and billions of years later our solar system and planet earth came into existence. Microscopic forms of life, unicellular organisms, only appeared on earth twelve billion years after the big bang; but in the relatively short three billion years until the present time, life forms in great abundance and complexity have populated the earth. How did this happen? Why has there come about this extraordinary organization of inanimate matter, first into life and then into rational life with all its various forms of cultural organization? If one simply appeals to the self-organizing properties of matter apart from spirit, is this not begging the question: isn't it precisely the nature of spirit to be the internal organizing principle of matter, something already functioning in matter from the very beginning of cosmic evolution but increasing in scope and intensity as time goes on?

Scientists, however, are reluctant to admit the possibility of outside (e.g., divine) intervention at any specific point in the evolutionary process. If, then, spirit is indeed present in matter, it must somehow be emergent out of matter and at least to some extent be controlled by empirically established conditions at the time of its emergence. Here the field-oriented approach to Whiteheadian societies mentioned above might be quite useful for interpreting this phenomenon of the emergence of spirit in progressively more organized forms out of preexistent matter. As noted already in chapters 5 and 6, fields (unlike substances or conventional "things") can be layered inside one another with the lower-level fields (e.g., at the atomic or molecular levels) supporting the operation of higher-level fields (e.g., at the organic and supra-organic [communitarian or environmental] levels of operation). But at the same time the higher-level fields of activity through the interplay of their more complex constituent actual occasions can exercise top-down causality on the functioning of the lower-level fields of activity.

Application to the Mind-Body Problem

The human mind, for example, as the topmost field of activity within the human being at every moment receives input from the brain and the other organs of the body. Then in responding to all that empirical data through its own subjective focus here and now, what Whitehead calls a

---

[16] See, e.g., Ian G. Barbour, *Religion and Science: Historical and Contemporary Issues* (San Francisco: HarperCollins, 1997), 107.

"regnant," or dominant, actual occasion,[17] it transmits a unified pattern of activity or "common element of form" to the rest of the body. But the lower-level fields of activity within the human body (e.g., at the atomic, molecular, and cellular levels of operation) through the activity of their constituent actual occasions exercise bottom-up or efficient causality upon the functioning of the brain and the mind as higher-level fields of activity. In this way, the brain and the mind are constrained in their operation by the current physical condition of the body. Thus there is spirit present at every level of existence and activity within the human body, but likewise matter is present in the form of progressively more complex fields of activity for the self-constitution of all the actual occasions or momentary subjects of experience thus involved.

Moreover, given this ongoing interchange between spirit and matter within the human body, it is relatively easy to imagine how the hierarchy of structured fields of activity and their constituent actual occasions within nature as a whole could have gradually emerged. As the saying goes, ontogeny recapitulates phylogeny; the structure of the individual organism reflects the growth of structure within the world around it. Initially, there were only atomic levels of existence and activity within nature. But with the slow growth of complexity within those same fields eventually a structure or "common element of form" appropriate to the molecular level of existence and activity emerged; with that structure came a more complex set of actual occasions capable of assimilating that pattern and perpetuating it. Then with the slow buildup of structure at the molecular level of existence and activity, the moment came for the formation of the first cells as a still higher-level field of activity for actual occasions within nature. Unicellular organisms were in due time succeeded by multicellular organisms that over time developed into the different species of life on the face of the earth at this time.

Thus the passage from non-life to life within nature was made through a gradual increase in complexity for the actual occasions involved at each level of existence and activity. When the moment was ripe, a new collective structure and a more complex set of actual occasions always emerged so as to constitute a still higher level of existence and activity within nature. There was no need for divine intervention so as to facilitate this passage from one level of existence and activity to another. The three divine persons, to be sure, were active in this process through provision of what Whitehead calls "divine initial aims" to the constituent actual

---

[17] Whitehead, *Process and Reality*, 103, 107–8.

occasions at every level within nature (see above, chap. 5). But between the subjects of experience at the inanimate and at the animate levels of existence and activity, there is even today only a difference in degree of complexity, not of basic design or "kind."[18] Spirit is present everywhere in nature; it is only a matter of its degree of self-organization and complexity.

Belief in Life after Death

Now we can consider how this scheme for the dynamic interrelation of spirit and matter can be of assistance to Christian philosophers and theologians in reconciling their basic religious beliefs with the reigning assumptions of modern science. Among those beliefs that are questionable in the face of contemporary scientific research, for example, is Christian belief in personal immortality and the resurrection of the body. From a strictly scientific perspective, the physical universe will in all likelihood end in either a "deep freeze" as a result of overexpansion or in a "heat death" as a result of contraction to a cosmic "singularity" all over again. On what rational basis, then, can Christians look forward to life after death together with the overall transformation of the physical universe in terms of a "new heaven and a new earth" as promised in Sacred Scripture (Rev 21:1)?

In line with the notion of panentheism as sketched above (see chaps. 5, 6, and 8), all creatures exist within and contribute to the structure of the divine matrix, the field of activity proper to the divine persons, during their time in this world. If the field of activity proper to each creature is then progressively being incorporated into the overall structure of that same divine matrix, then objective immortality within the divine life is already assured not only for human beings but for all other creatures as well. What we human beings, for example, think, say, and do at every moment of our lives is even now being "recorded" within the divine matrix and preserved until we take conscious possession of our personal field of activity at the moment of death.

The key idea here, of course, is that if there is "matter" in a qualified sense even within God, then matter must be such that it can be incorporated into and thereby preserved within the divine life. Admittedly, what we conventionally perceive as matter with our senses is somewhat il-

---

[18] Ibid., 177–78.

lusory. It is not something solid and inert. According to contemporary natural science, matter is simply energy shaped or formed in such a way as to become the persons and things of common sense experience. In terms of my own understanding of the God-world relationship, matter is a set of interrelated energy fields structured by the events taking place within them, the interrelated "decisions" of all the actual occasions in existence at any given moment. In this way, matter and spirit are interdependent. Matter is just as "immaterial" as spirit, and spirit is just as "material" as matter.

Yet even if we grant that everything that happens in this world is somehow recorded within the divine life, how does one explain subjective immortality, the way in which human beings (and presumably other living creatures as well) can experience life after death, or resurrection? As I have explained elsewhere in greater detail,[19] this full incorporation into the divine life does indeed require a special intervention on the part of the divine persons. Subjective immortality is their gift to us rather than something we deserve. Yet in terms of our understanding of the interrelation of matter and spirit, it can be explained as follows. The final set of actual occasions or momentary subjects of experience at work within the mind and body of a human being at the moment of death will not only be objectively incorporated into the divine matrix as in previous moments of existence but (in a way that we here and now cannot understand scientifically) will be transformed and elevated so as to enjoy subjective immortality within the divine life as well. This represents, to be sure, a break with the laws of nature as we currently understand them. But since it is a divine intervention taking place only at the moment of death or passage out of this life, it does not interfere with the operation of the laws of nature within this life.

The End of the World and the Transformation of the Universe

Likewise, if we believe that the human body can be thus transformed so as to enjoy subjective immortality, then the rest of the physical universe should likewise (once again in a way unknown to us here and now) be capable of analogous transformation and full incorporation within the divine life. Not everything will be conscious of its new mode of existence

---

[19] See, e.g., Bracken, *The One in the Many*, 157–78; likewise, "Intersubjectivity and the Coming of God," in *Journal of Religion* 83 (2003): 381–400.

within the life proper to the three divine persons since much that exists in this life here and now does not possess consciousness or self-awareness (e.g., all inanimate things). But if it is true that our bodies are microcosms of the universe, composed of the same atoms and molecules as everything else that exists in this world, then something akin to resurrection is in store for our world as a whole. In effect, nothing that comes into existence within the divine life ever completely perishes; somehow everything survives. But it survives only because from its very beginnings in the mind of God, it was always a combination of spirit and matter.

Conclusion

What I have done then in the preceding paragraphs is to indicate how natural scientists, on the one hand, and philosopher/theologians, on the other hand, can use the same basic terms, matter and spirit, with at least somewhat the same meaning, within their respective disciplines. This may seem like a very modest gain in terms of sustaining the dialogue between the proponents of religion and science. But it is a necessary first step in constructing a mutually satisfactory worldview. Aristotle in his day had a uniform understanding of "matter" and "form" that worked equally well in writing both the *Metaphysics* (the equivalent of his treatise on theology or the God-world relationship) and treatises on the phenomena of nature (e.g., the *Physics*, the treatise *On the Soul*, etc.).[20] The same was true of Thomas Aquinas and other medieval philosopher/theologians, given their adaptation of Aristotle's metaphysics to legitimate specifically Christian beliefs like creation out of nothing (*creatio ex nihilo*). As we have seen in chapter 3, however, the ancient and medieval worldview collapsed, or at least became highly questionable, under the impact of the discoveries of early modern science in the West. Furthermore, up to the present there has arisen no fully satisfactory replacement for the classical worldview.

Accordingly, something must be done in our time to facilitate better communication between philosophers and theologians, on the one hand, and natural and social scientists, on the other hand. For this reason, the right kind of relationship between religion and science is perhaps more important than all the other issues discussed in this book. It is the one

---

[20] See, e.g., W. T. Jones, *A History of Western Philosophy*, 2nd ed. (New York: Harcourt, Brace & World, 1969): I, 214–54.

issue most needing careful reflection and discussion by Christians and members of the other world religions. For if religion functions in virtual independence of science, it often degenerates into beliefs and practices harmful to society at large.[21] Likewise, if science pays no attention to the classical values embodied in the beliefs and practices of the various world religions, it too poses a threat to the continued well-being of the broader community.[22] Hence, the fashioning of a new worldview that would be generally acceptable to representatives of both religion and science would seem to be the most pressing long-range issue of our times. The point of this chapter and indeed much of this book has been to suggest that such a new worldview is perhaps slowly taking shape (see Polkinghorne's comments at the beginning of this chapter). If so, it will presumably be an ontology or metaphysics with heavy emphasis on the interconnectedness and interdependence of everything on everything else. For Christians this new worldview could readily be supported by a rethinking of the classical doctrine of the Trinity so as to endorse the social model for the Trinity that emphasizes the interdependence of the divine persons both with one another and with all their creatures (see chap. 6).

Furthermore, if this specifically trinitarian approach to a relational worldview is generally accepted by Christians, then it will surely update and improve the older Christian worldview based on the philosophy of Aristotle and Aquinas. For the explanation of the doctrine of the Trinity in Aquinas's *Summa Theologiae* was evidently more an exception to than an integral part of his overall approach to the God-world relationship in the *Summa Theologiae*. But if this new relational approach to the world of nature is likewise compatible with a relational understanding of the doctrine of the Trinity, then at least among Christians there is good reason for excitement and enthusiasm. The separate worlds of God, humanity, and nature are once again brought into dynamic interrelation as in the classical worldview, but on a much richer conceptual basis so as to allow for still further growth and development in the future. Such a "cosmo-theandric" synthesis (see chap. 8) should then fully restore the doctrine

---

[21] Think, for example, how much violence in today's world is carried out by individuals convinced that they are doing God's will and are thus not bound by the natural law.

[22] Contemporary science is heavily linked at present to expensive technology with corresponding dependence on government or business sources for funding. Scientists, accordingly, may be tempted to set aside persistent ethical issues arising out of their research so as better to compete for funding or even personal profit (e.g., the felt need at present to acquire patents on chemically altered genes).

of the Trinity to its rightful place in Christian theology as the point of origin and the ultimate goal of salvation history, the *raison d'être* for the entire cosmic process from a Christian perspective.

Conclusion

Looking back on the preceding chapters of this book, we can readily see how far we have come in trying to understand and appreciate our common Christian belief in the doctrine of the Trinity, three persons and yet one God. As we saw in the first chapter, the initial followers of Jesus, who as faithful Jews were firm believers in God as One, were faced with a major problem in accounting for their experience of the risen Jesus as likewise divine, thus on a par with God as his heavenly father. Likewise, they had vivid experiences, both as individuals and as community members, of the Holy Spirit as a dynamic personal presence in their lives. How to reconcile belief in God as one with their personal and corporate experience of God as three distinct "personalities" was the major preoccupation of reflective Christians well into the fourth century. Even after the Council of Nicaea and the First Council of Constantinople seemed to settle the issue, at least provisionally, theologians in both East and West continued to work on a rational explanation of this core Christian belief. Yet because there was so little communication between the Western Church under the rule of the Pope and the Eastern Church under the leadership of the Patriarch of Constantinople, effectively two different approaches to the doctrine developed, with the Western Church emphasizing the reality of God as One and the Eastern Church the reality of God as three distinct persons.

In the third chapter we noted how, at least in the West, the doctrine of the Trinity gradually faded in importance for the faithful. This was partly due to the highly speculative and abstract explanations of the doctrine put forth by Aquinas and other medieval thinkers. But it was also due to the influence of a number of medieval mystics, like Meister Eckhart in Germany and the unknown author of *The Cloud of Unknowing* in England, who emphasized the incomprehensibility of God and/or the mysterious reality of the Godhead or the divine nature. Furthermore, beginning with Nicholas of Cusa and his emphasis on the divine infinity and God as "the coincidence of opposites," attention was given more and more to the world of nature in which the reality of God was thought to be imperfectly reflected. But this line of thought only demanded belief in God as One, the divine Architect of the world as a smoothly running cosmic machine. The image of such a distant God, however, soon yielded in the minds of many scientists and other educated people to virtual agnosticism about the existence of God and God's relation to the world of nature and then for some even to outspoken atheism. Will not science, after all, eventually solve all our human problems? What need is there for a Creator God?

Yet, in truly amazing fashion, interest in the doctrine of the Trinity rebounded dramatically in the twentieth century. Beginning with the appeal of Karl Barth to return to the Bible as the sole source of our human knowledge of God, theologians such as Karl Rahner and Eberhard Jüngel in Europe and Catherine Mowry LaCugna in the United States sought to ground Christian belief and practice in a consciously trinitarian world-view. The Trinity must be the starting point for both prayer and rational reflection. One should pray not simply to God in general but to Father, Son, and Holy Spirit in particular. Likewise, in thinking through how to reconcile belief in God as both transcendent and immanent, that is, as both beyond the world of space and time and yet intimately involved in what is happening in this world, these same theologians had to think through many of the traditional attributes of God (e.g., God as infinite, all-powerful, all-knowing) and ask themselves what needed to be modified in order to make sense to Christians in an increasingly secular world.

It is no surprise, then, that as part of this renaissance of interest in the doctrine of the Trinity among theologians and other educated Christians in the twentieth century a wide spectrum of new perspectives sprang up, some of which we analyzed in chapters 5 to 8. In line with a new interest in the Scripture texts portraying Jesus as fully human as well as divine, for example, scholars began to question whether God in any sense "suffers" as a result of first creating and then guiding an imperfect world. As we saw in chapter 5, European scholars like Jürgen Moltmann and Paul Fiddes who experienced the trauma of World War II felt impelled to claim that it is not just Jesus in his human nature but the triune God as a whole who feels the pain of this world and works to relieve it. Another European-born thinker, Alfred North Whitehead, thinking more in terms of a totally new process-oriented worldview, likewise claimed that God is clearly participant in the cosmic process, being as much affected by the ups and downs of life in this world as genuinely affecting the cosmic process through the constant provision of divine "initial aims" to creatures.

For many of the same reasons, Moltmann as well as Colin Gunton, Wolfhart Pannenberg, and the Latin American liberation theologian Leonardo Boff came up with a new pastoral approach to the inner life of God. God is a community of divine persons who in their ongoing dynamic interrelation provide a model for justice and equality among human beings in their secular and religious communities. My own contribution to this discussion was to make clear how Alfred North Whitehead's understanding of the God-world relationship can be revised to allow for the inclusion of all the works of creation within the all-embracing field of activity or ground of being constituted by the divine persons in their dynamic interrelation. The divine persons, therefore, are not only an enduring model of community life simply for human beings; they are the archetypal community that incorporates all the finite communities of this world within its infinitely extended field of activity and thereby makes possible eternal life not only for human beings but for all other creatures in proportion to their ability to experience new life.

In chapters 7 and 8 we reviewed serious objections to the classical understanding of the doctrine of the Trinity from two quite different perspectives. With her incisive critique of an all-pervasive patriarchy within traditional Christianity, Mary Daly made clear in *Beyond God the Father* that the exclusively male imagery used to describe the divine persons is destructive of female well-being and personal integrity. Hence, women must either renounce their allegiance to any form of institutional Christianity as Daly herself did or, in any event, seriously revise the classical understanding of God and the God-world relationship within Christianity as many other Christian feminists have done, often through appeal to a new egalitarian understanding of the doctrine of the Trinity. Then in chapter 8 we worked with the notable hypothesis of S. Mark Heim about a potential plurality of religious "ends" or forms of salvation so as to indicate how the doctrine of the Trinity might in a curious way serve as a model for understanding the relation of the world religions to one another. That is, just as the divine persons are distinctively themselves only in terms of their ongoing relations of opposition to one another, so the world religions only make full sense in terms of their doctrinal differences vis-à-vis one another. Thus, if the one God must be three distinct but interrelated persons, then Ultimate Reality will be fully comprehensible only in terms of harmonizing the rival claims of all the major world religions.

Finally, in chapter 9 we projected a possible future for the doctrine of the Trinity in terms of the ever-expanding dialogue between religion and science in our time. More and more the deliberate isolation of the sciences and the humanities from one another, which we described in chapter 3, is being called into question. Scientists are seeing the limits of the mechanistic worldview endorsed by Galileo, Newton, and other early modern natural scientists. Relativity theory and quantum field theory in physics, the phenomenon of the unexpected "emergence" of new forms in contemporary chemistry and biology, all mutely appeal for a new and more comprehensive worldview in which the relation between spirit and matter will be dramatically reconceived and redefined. Likewise, philosophers and theologians in large numbers are currently speculating about panentheism, which is intermediate between the implicit dualism of classical metaphysics and some form of pantheism, as a useful model of the God-world relationship. Here the notion of the Trinity as a community of divine persons who through the gift of creation have extended their communitarian life to a wide range of creatures is very attractive. God, after all, must be seen as simultaneously the Creator of the cosmic process and a full participant within it. How else are we Christians to conceive this approach to the God-world relationship except in terms of the Trinity, one of whose person-members became human and through his life, death, and resurrection drew all his fellow human beings and indeed the whole of material creation into the intimacy of the divine life?

But in the final analysis we have to admit that the continuing vitality of the doctrine of the Trinity lies not so much in rational reflection (new approaches to the God-world relationship) but in praise and worship (prayer on both an individual and a collective basis). In the words of Martin Buber, God should be spoken to rather than spoken about, addressed as Thou rather than He, She, or It. As we mentioned in the introduction to this book, the study of theology is seldom, if ever, purely academic. After all, one is probing into the ultimate meaning and value of one's life, even though Ultimate Reality (for Christians, the triune God) remains forever mysterious and beyond full human comprehension. An act of faith in some form or other will then always be necessary to bridge the gap between the finite and the infinite. Yet no decision that one makes in the course of a lifetime is more important for one's self-identity or sense of purpose in life. It is my hope that this modest book will offer to the reader some guidance in making such an important decision and then abiding by it.

Further Reading

Baker-Fletcher, Karen. *Dancing with God: The Trinity from a Womanist Perspective.* St. Louis, MO: Chalice Press, 2006.

Bell, David N. *A Cloud of Witnesses: An Introductory History of the Development of Christian Doctrine to 500 AD.* Kalamazoo, MI: Cistercian Publications, 1989.

Bracken, Joseph A. *The Triune Symbol: Persons, Process, and Community.* Lanham, MD: University Press of America, 1985.

D'Costa, Gavin. *The Meeting of Religions and the Trinity.* Maryknoll, NY: Orbis, 2000.

Edwards, Denis. *Breath of Life: A Theology of the Creator Spirit.* Maryknoll, NY: Orbis, 2004.

———. *The God of Evolution: A Trinitarian Theology.* New York: Paulist, 1999.

Fatula, Mary Ann. *The Triune God of Christian Faith.* Collegeville, MN: Liturgical Press, 1990.

Fiddes, Paul. *Participating in God: A Pastoral Doctrine of the Trinity.* Louisville, KY: Westminster/John Knox, 2000.

Grant, Robert M. *Gods and the One God.* Philadelphia: Westminster, 1986.

Grenz, Stanley J. *The Social God and the Relational Self: A Trinitarian Theology of the Imago Dei.* Louisville, KY: Westminster/John Knox, 2001.

Gunton, Colin. *The Triune Creator: A Historical and Systematic Study.* Grand Rapids, MI: Eerdmans, 1998.

Hodgson, Leonard. *The Doctrine of the Trinity.* New York: Scribner's, 1944.

Hunt, Anne. *Trinity: Nexus of the Mysteries of Christian Faith.* Maryknoll, NY: Orbis, 2005.

———. *What Are They Saying about the Trinity?* New York: Paulist, 1998.

Lee, Jung Young. *The Trinity in Asian Perspective.* Nashville, TN: Abingdon, 1996.

Lorenzen, Lynne Faber. *The College Student's Introduction to the Trinity.* Collegeville, MN: Liturgical Press, 1999.

Maloney, George. *Abiding in the Indwelling Trinity.* New York: Paulist, 2004.

Marshall, Bruce. *Trinity and Truth.* Cambridge, UK: Cambridge University Press, 2000.

Moltmann, Jürgen. *History and the Triune God.* New York: Crossroad, 1992.

Norris, Richard A. *God and World in Early Christian Theology.* New York: Seabury, 1965.

O'Donnell, John J. *The Mystery of the Triune God.* New York: Paulist, 1989.

———. *Trinity and Temporality: The Christian Doctrine of God in the Light of Process Theology and the Theology of Hope.* New York: Oxford University Press, 1983.

O'Collins, Gerald. *The Tripersonal God: Understanding and Interpreting the Trinity.* New York: Paulist, 1999.

Ogbonnaya, A. Okechukwa. *On Communitarian Divinity: An African Interpretation of the Trinity.* New York: Paragon House, 1994.

Pelikan, Jaroslav. *The Christian Tradition: Vol I [The Emergence of the Catholic Tradition].* Chicago: University of Chicago Press, 1972.

———. *The Christian Tradition: Vol II [The Spirit of Eastern Christendom].* Chicago: University of Chicago Press, 1974.

Wainwright, Geoffrey. *Doxology: The Praise of God in Worship, Doctrine and Life.* New York: Oxford University Press, 1980.

Welsh, Claude. *In This Name: The Doctrine of the Trinity in Contemporary Theology.* New York: Scribner's, 1952.

Zizioulas, John. *Being as Communion.* Crestwood, NY: St. Vladimir's Seminary Press, 1993.

———. *Communion and Otherness: Further Studies in Personhood and Church.* Edited by Paul McPartlan. New York: T&T Clark, 2006.

NB: These works on the doctrine of the Trinity were not mentioned either in the text or endnotes of this book but are worthy of mention, if only because they offer further evidence of the wide range of literature on the subject of the Trinity within the past half-century.

Index of Names and Topics